BROKEN GLORY

THE FINAL YEARS OF ROBERT F. KENNEDY

ED SANDERS · RICK VEITCH

A GRAPHIC HISTORY

Arcade Publishing • New York

First Edition

Lyrics from "Crucifixion" by Phil Ochs © by Barricade Music, Inc., reprinted by permission

Arcade Publishing books may be purchased in bulk at special discounts for sales promotion, corporate gifts, fund-raising, or educational purposes. Special editions can also be created to specifications. For details, contact the Special Sales Department, Arcade Publishing, 307 West 36th Street, 11th Floor, New York, NY 10018 or arcade@skyhorsepublishing.com.

Arcade Publishing® is a registered trademark of Skyhorse Publishing, Inc.®, a Delaware corporation.

Visit our website at www.arcadepub.com.
Visit Rick Veitch's website at www.rickveitch.com.

10 9 8 7 6 5 4 3 2 1

Library of Congress Cataloging-in-Publication Data is available.
Library of Congress Control Number: 2017963142

Cover design by Erin Seaward-Hiatt
Cover illustration: Rick Veitch

ISBN: 978-1-62872-951-1
Ebook ISBN: 978-1-62872-952-8

Printed in China

"Time takes her toll and the memory fades
but his glory is broken, in the magic that he made . . . "

—Phil Ochs, "Crucifixion"

"The wicked persecute the good
with the blindness of the passion that animates them,
while the good pursue the wicked with a wise discretion."

—St. Augustine

"One's file, you know, is never quite complete; a case
is never really closed, even after a century, when all
the participants are dead."

—Graham Greene, *The Third Man*

"I would be an historian as Herodotus was,
looking for oneself for the evidence of what is said."

—Charles Olson

Introduction
by Ed Sanders

What a calamity to American history was the murder of Robert Kennedy! How different would the course of the United States have been if a rogue and powerful group had not killed, and covered up his murder, and the murders of John Kennedy and Martin Luther King, Jr. as well.

I began researching and compiling files on the Robert Kennedy assassination during my work in early 1970s for my book *The Family*, about the Manson group, published in 1971. Then in 1972, my investigative associate, Larry Larsen, who had helped me research the book, reported from a law enforcement source about the possibility of a connection between Manson and the murder of someone, Larsen told me, because of her knowledge of "something she was not supposed to overhear either in regards to Sirhan Sirhan or about Sirhan."

By 1974, I had learned even more and decided to write a poem about the final years of Robert Kennedy. I worked on and off on RFK for the next six years. Beginning in 1980, I turned to other researches and projects, setting aside the Kennedy poem, though I had collected around 4,000 pages of FBI files, and several bankers boxes of sleuthery into the case.

Over the years, I always looked for, then clipped and filed whatever information and articles would appear about RFK and the ongoing investigations of his murder but busied myself with writing books such as my collected poems, *Thirsting for Peace in a Raging Century*, and various recording projects for my band, The Fugs, plus books such as *Chekhov, 1968: A History in Verse*, and *The Poetry and Life of Allen Ginsberg*. I also wrote two new editions of *The Family*, in 1990 and in 2002.

Beginning in the 1980s and 1990s, much important new information has been made available to the public. For instance, in 1988 the California State Archives received voluminous files, tapes, photos and official reports, previously unread by the public, from the Los Angeles Police Department's investigation of the RFK shooting. That same year, the large Robert F. Kennedy Assassination Archive (RFKAA) at the University of Massachusetts Dartmouth was assembled by author and professor of political science Philip Melanson and the RFK Assassination Archive Committee of the University Library. Original materials, including research files, audiotape interviews, videotapes and news clippings were donated in several installments by a number of private individuals investigating the case. To this core collection were added thousands of pages of FBI documents, released by the Freedom of Information Act to the university, between 1984 and 1986.

All of this voluminous information was very useful when, in 2008, for the fortieth anniversary of RFK's murder, I wrote a poem about the final day, June 4, 1968. After that I continued work on the RFK project, which has grown over the decades to over fifteen bankers boxes of investigative files, and has resulted in the text of *Broken Glory: The Final Years of Robert F. Kennedy.*

During these years, I also wrote a biography of the actress Sharon Tate, which was published in 2016. The noted artist Rick Veitch drew brilliant illustrations for my biography of Tate, and then Veitch began creating illustrations for *Broken Glory: The Final Years of Robert F. Kennedy.*

Robert Kennedy was shot and killed just minutes after giving his victory speech in a hotel ballroom after winning the California Democratic presidential primary in Los Angeles. It was a humble and positive speech. Kennedy had more campaigning to do, but he realized that the Presidency was well within his reach, and that he could then have a big impact on war and peace, on racial justice, on a fair economic shake for all the people, and to bring to justice at last to those who had killed John F. Kennedy.

RFK was a remarkable American leader, forged in the Civil Rights struggle while he was US attorney general during John Kennedy's administration, and then later, as a senator, involved in the eye-opening, ever-growing challenge to halt the war in Vietnam, his work against apartheid, and unselfish activism for prosperity for all humans. He was a great and inspirational candidate, forged in the tragedy and suffering about which Aeschylus wrote, in a religious context, that it would fall drop by drop upon the heart "until in our own despair, against our will, comes wisdom through the awful grace of God."

The future will bring forth the full story of RFK's martyrdom. May this book of text and illuminating illustrations help heal this half-century wound in the body politic of the United States. I am certain that there exists out there information for further elucidation, perhaps in dusty research transfile boxes kept in the loft of a garage, or in long-unused filing cabinets—may this book help inspire that this information be brought forward into the "hard Sophoclean light."

Note on Sources

I have used information in the text of *Broken Glory* from a large number of sources, particularly from outstanding researchers such as Philip Melanson, William Turner, Jonn Christian, Lynn Mangan, and Lisa Pease. I have also utilized material from the court filings of attorneys William Pepper and Laurie Dusek on behalf of Sirhan Sirhan, particularly reports by Dr. Daniel P. Brown, Associate Clinical Professor in Psychology at Harvard Medical School, who wrote reports for Sirhan's defense based upon his hypnosis of Sirhan Sirhan over a number of years. Dr. Brown's reports, for instance, presented claims by Sirhan Sirhan that he had been programmed during the days leading up to Robert Kennedy's assassination by a person or persons with whom Sirhan had been communicating over a ham radio set located in Sirhan's home in Pasadena.

Salute to RFK Researchers

There have been a good number of researchers and tireless seekers after the truth about the killing of Robert Kennedy, who have done remarkable work over the years. Key among these are Philip Melanson, Greg Stone, Allard Lowenstein, William Turner, Jonn Christian; Lillian Castellano and Floyd Nelson of the CTKA (Citizens for Truth about the Kennedy Assassination); Bud Fensterwald of the Committee to Investigate Assassinations, Vincent Bugliosi, William Harper, Ted Charach, Betsy Langman, Alexander Cockburn, Shane O'Sullivan, Baxter Ward, Larry Larsen, Peter Noyes, Paul Schrade, William Pepper, Laurie Dusek, Dr. Daniel Brown, Alan Scheflin, Jim DiEugenio, Mary Ferrell, Donald Bain, Donald Freed, Dr. Eduard Simson-Kallas, Jim Kostman, Mae Brussell, James Lesar, Robert Blair Kaiser, Rush Harp, Walter Bowart, Robert Cutler, Richard Sprague; Jeff Cohen, Judith Farrar, Carl Oglesby, Bob Katz and Martin Lee of the Assassination Information Bureau, great researcher Lynn Mangan, Lawrence Teeter, Lisa Pease and others.

Thanks

Thanks to Larry Larsen, Martin Lee, Paul Fitzgerald, Peter Noyes, Miriam Sanders, Donald Freed, Tom Pacheco, Maury Terry, Bob Katz, Carl Oglesby,

Alexander Cockburn, Vincent Bugliosi, William Turner, Carl George, Barry Farrell, Robert Cutler, Mae Brussell, Robert Blair Kaiser, Andrea Wyatt, Bud Fensterwald, John Rose, Rush Harp, Duncan Harp, William Pepper, Frank Morales, Judith Farrar of the RFK Assassination Archives at UMass Dartmouth, Nick Lyons and others for help in researching this book and helping its publication.

Also, a life-long thanks to my bardic mentors, Charles Olson and Allen Ginsberg.

BROKEN GLORY

THE FINAL YEARS OF ROBERT F. KENNEDY

"Wisdom comes through the awful grace of God."

Jackie after November 22

Jackie had urged him to read
Edith Hamilton's *The Greek Way*
(which had just come out in paperback)
not long after JFK's visit to Dallas.

He read it carefully, also Hamilton's *Three Greek Plays*,

and he became fascinated with Aeschylus,
who believed most fervently
in the fierce shaping of humanity
on the fate-beating forge of earned & unearned suffering

till "wisdom comes
through the awful grace of God."

JFK Talks about His Own Assassination And That of Robert Kennedy Also

November 22, in their hotel suite in Fort Worth
in the morning,

the President read a full-page ad
in the *Dallas Morning News*
addressed to him.
It was bordered in black.

"WELCOME MR. KENNEDY. Because of your
policy, thousands of Cubans have been imprisoned,
are starving and being persecuted—with thousands
already murdered and thousands more awaiting execution
and, in addition, the entire population of almost
7,000,000 Cubans are living in slavery.

"Why have you approved the sale of wheat
and corn to our enemies when you know the Communist
soldiers 'travel on their stomachs' just as ours do?
Communist soldiers are daily wounding and/or killing
American soldiers in South Viet Nam."

JFK handed the ad to his wife, who read it
and he said,
>   "We're heading into nut country today.
>   But Jackie, if somebody wants to shoot me
>   from a window with a rifle,
>   nobody can stop it, so why worry
>   about it?

"You know," said JFK, "last night would have been
a hell of a night to assassinate a president. I mean it.
There was the rain, and the night,
>   and we were all getting jostled.
>   Suppose a man had a pistol in a briefcase."

>   The President aimed his right hand,
>   as if it were a pistol,
>   at the wall, his thumb
>   serving as a hammer.

>   "Then he could have dropped the gun and the
>   briefcase, and melted away in the crowd."

JFK just before his final motorcade
had described his own murder
& 4 1/2 years later RFK's
>   jostled by the crowd in the pantry.[1]

Kennedy Family Message to the Kremlin

In early December 1963
Robert Kennedy and Jacqueline Kennedy
sent a trusted family friend,
>   William Walton,
to deliver a secret message
to the Soviet leadership
on what the Kennedys considered
>   the true cause of the assassination—

that there was a right-wing conspiracy
behind the guns of Dallas

& that RFK
>   would seek higher office

2

"We're heading into nut country today."

& would eventually
                    seek the Presidency

to continue the voyage of peace
            JFK had begun.[2]

Possibly Running for Vice President

One burning issue in 1964
        had RFK running for vice president under LBJ.

        An April '64 Gallup poll:
        48% for RFK 18% for Stevenson
                        10% for Hubert Humphrey.[3]

        When Goldwater won the Republican nomination
        as a fairly ultra-rightist

        LBJ felt he no longer needed RFK
                            on the ticket.[4]

Hickory Hill

Hickory Hill had been the headquarters of the Union Army
during the Civil War—a large, white-hued mansion
in the "rolling country" of McLean, Virginia.

Robert and Ethel had moved into it in '55.

It was near CIA headquarters.

Hickory Hill had been originally built in 1810,
stood on a slight hill with lawns on the slopes,
with a tennis court and a pool with a bath house.

        The house had emblems of history:
        Lincoln's Emancipation Proclamation
                        mounted on an easel
                                in the den.
        On tables: autographed pictures of Herbert Hoover,
        Konrad Adenauer, Winston Churchill.

Hickory Hill

On a wall JFK's Inaugural Address inscribed to Bobby

& near the entry to the house
a letter from FDR to RFK, then 14, complimenting him
on his stamp collecting hobby, and inviting him
            to the White House to view FDR's own collection.[5]

Runs for Senate from New York
August 22, 1964

Robert Kennedy announced his candidacy for
        US Senator from New York

His brother Edward had suffered a horrid plane crash
                        the previous June
& had caused Robert to consider leaving politics,

but then the wild reception he'd felt
            traveling to Europe
                    made him realize he could not give up
                    JFK's Dream.[6]

        Robert Kennedy won the Senate race
        & was sworn in on January 4, 1965.[7]

Doubts on Vietnam

His doubts about the wisdom of the War Caste's
            Vietnam war
                    & the ever-increasing aerial bombing
                            with napalm and defoliation
                    started slowly, then grew and grew.

Kennedy went to South America in the fall o' '65
and praised Johnson's leadership in 'Nam

and talked about the US's difficulties
            in securing peace in Southeast Asia.[8]

Senate run

December 5, 1965, Kennedy was asked on *Meet the Press*
if he favored halting the bombing of North Vietnam
in order to bring about negotiations.

RFK said yes to this.

He said that military parts of the strife
were being excessively emphasized
over economics & politics.

1965 December,
184,300 US troops in 'Nam.[9]

Johnson had ordered a holiday bombing pause
around Christmas of '65.

There was much debate
whether it should continue
including a meeting with leaders
of Congress on January 20,

then on January 25 ordered it to resume.[10]

February '66,
the Senate Foreign Relations Committee
held two weeks of hearings on Vietnam.

RFK was very attentive to those hearings,
several times watched them
as a spectator in the room.

Then prepared his own statement,
which he made on February 19
just before leaving on a skiing trip
with his family.

He said, "There are three routes available
to the United States
in its involvement in Vietnam—
military victory, unilateral withdrawal, or
a peaceful settlement."

Haiphong harbor bombed

The only way to move forward
was a negotiated settlement

with the National Liberation Front
                    (The Viet Cong)
to recognize "the fact that there are
discontented elements in South Vietnam,
Communist and non-Communist, who desire
to change the existing political
                    and economic system of the country."

These elements, argued RFK,
must be brought in
        for a "share of power and responsibility"
in a successful negotiated settlement
                    to end the military battles.[11]

Key administration officials such as
VP Hubert Humphrey
        & McGeorge Bundy

spoke against bringing the NLF
                    into negotiations.

RFK sought to minimize the
        differences with LBJ
but the media puffed them up.

        He was now committed
        to a political resolution
                    & negotiation
                        to resolve
                        the Vietnamese Conflict.[12]

In June 1966
Johnson and the Military
        added Haiphong harbor
                to the bombing targets

RFK issued a statement
which challenged the step
        to retard North Vietnam's ability
        to send supplies to the Viet Cong.

Cape Town

"Unfortunately," wrote Kennedy, "past escalations
have been accompanied by assurances that this
would be the case. Those predictions,
as most concerning Vietnam
      in the last twenty years,
            have been wrong."

Two of Johnson's good friends,
      Senators Mike Mansfield and William Fulbright,

      strongly opposed LBJ on Vietnam.[13]

Robert Kennedy's Powerful
Speech in South Africa
June 6, 1966

In the fall of 1965 a medical student invited Senator Kennedy to
deliver the annual Day of Affirmation of Academic
      and Human Freedom speech at the University of Cape Town.

RFK accepted but the apartheid gov't stalled for months
granting a visa
      and finally giving it for only four days.

On June 4, Robert and Ethel, plus RFK's secretary Angie Novello
      and RFK staff member Adam Walinsky
      flew to Johannesburg
      greeted by a big crowd at the airport.

June 5 to Pretoria where prime minister Verwoerd
        refused to see the Senator.

June 6 to Cape Town to deliver the speech,
      with 3,000 greeting him at the airport.

      Adam Walinsky had written a draft back in DC.
      Allard Lowenstein read it, and urged he make it stronger.
      Richard Goodwin was asked to help
        and the speech was finalized.

      RFK went over it one more time
        on the way to Cape Town University

"At the heart of that Western freedom and democracy
is the belief that the individual man, the child of God,
is the touchstone of value."

where there were 18,000 on hand to greet RFK
& shout and cheer his words—

RFK biographer Arthur Schlesinger, Jr.
judged it "Kennedy's greatest speech."

He began: "I come here this evening because of my
deep interest and affection for a land settled by the Dutch
in the mid-seventeenth century, then taken over by the British,
and at last independent; a land in which the native inhabitants
were at first subdued, but relations with whom remain a problem
to this day; a land which defined itself on a hostile frontier;
a land which has tamed rich natural resources through the
energetic application of modern technology; a land which was
once the importer of slaves, and now must struggle
to wipe out the last traces of that former bondage.
            I refer, of course, to the United States of America.

"But I am glad to come here—and my wife and I and all of our party
are glad to come here to South Africa, and we're glad to come
to Cape Town. I am already greatly enjoying my stay and my visit
here. I am making an effort to meet and exchange views
with people of all walks of life, and all segments of South African
opinion, including those who represent
            the views of the government. . . .

"This is a Day of Affirmation, a celebration of liberty. We stand here
in the name of freedom. At the heart of that Western freedom
and democracy is the belief that the individual man,
            the child of God, is the touchstone of value, and all society,
all groups and states exist for that person's benefit.
Therefore, the enlargement of liberty for individual human beings
must be the supreme goal and the abiding practice
            of any Western society."

The speech continues for 8 full pages, ending as follows:

"So we part, I to my country and you to remain.
We are, if a man of 40 can claim the privilege,
fellow members of the world's largest younger generation.
Each of us have our own work to do. I know at times you must feel
very alone with your problems and with your difficulties.

14

Mandela

But I want to say how I—impressed I am with the stand—
with what you stand for and for the effort that you are making;
and I say this not just for myself, but men and women
all over the world. And I hope you will often take heart
from the knowledge that you are joined with your fellow young
people in every land, they struggling with their problems and you
with yours, but all joined in a common purpose; that,
like the young people of my own country and of every country
that I have visited, you are all in many ways more closely united
to the brothers of your time than to the older generations
in any of these nations. You're determined to build a better future.

"President Kennedy was speaking to the young people of America,
but beyond them to young people everywhere, when he said:
'The energy, the faith, the devotion which we bring to this endeavor
will light our country and all who serve it; and the glow from that fire
can truly light the world.' And, he added, 'With a good conscience
our only sure reward, with history the final judge of our deeds,
let us go forth to lead the land we love, asking His blessing and
His help, but knowing that here on earth God's work
                         must truly be our own.'"

The Senator spent his last day in Johannesburg, where he toured
    Soweto where 500,000 blacks lived hemmed in by
            wire fences through which they could enter & depart
                         after showing identity cards.

    Afterward, many placed pictures of RFK from the newspapers
            on the walls of their housing.[14]

Mandela

In prison on nearby Robben Island
was African National Congress leader Nelson Mandela

who would not be released for another 24 years
            after RFK's speech in Cape Town
with the final fall of Apartheid
            in 1990.

"I never thought it was the Cubans. If anyone was involved it was organized crime. But there's nothing I can do about it."

A Conversation about JFK Assassination

On July 25, 1966
    confidant Richard Goodwin
        had stayed at RFK's UN Plaza suite.

(Goodwin had been a speechwriter for John Kennedy
    and then an Assistant Secretary of State
                        for Latin American Affairs.
    He'd helped to create the Alliance For Progress,
    a Latin America economic development program,
            set up by JFK in '61, & helped write
            the recent speech in Cape Town.)

He'd just written a friendly review of
Edward Epstein's *Inquest: The Warren Commission and
                    the Establishment of Truth*,
which was the first book on the assassination
to make criticism of the Warren Commission "respectable"

& which suggested there was more than one gunman.

    During their discussions that evening
    Goodwin brought up JFK.
    RFK was very hesitant.
    Then Goodwin suggested hiring an investigator.

    "You might try Carmine Bellino," said Robert.
    "He's the best in the country."

    Later that night RFK said,
        "I never thought it was the Cubans.
        If anyone was involved it was organized crime.
                    But there's nothing I can do about it.

                Not now."[15]

President Charles de Gaulle of France
on September 2, 1966
                harshly denounced the American intervention
                    in Vietnam

but offered to mediate between the US & 'Nam,

an offer Johnson quickly rebuffed.[16]

A Young Man Who Wanted to Become a Jockey

He was a Christian Palestinian
and a citizen of Jordan,
born in Jerusalem on March 19, 1944.

When 12, he moved to the US with his family,
settling in California. Shortly thereafter his father
Bishara moved back to the Middle East.

In the 1960s, his mother Mary and her three sons lived in a small
house on East Howard Street in Pasadena.

Sirhan graduated from John Muir High School in Pasadena
& attended Pasadena City College.

He was a fan of the racetrack, slight of form,
& hungered to become a jockey.
In '66 he was working as a stable boy
for a trainer at Santa Anita Race Track
              named Gordon Bowsher

but was unhappy because Bowsher
only employed him as a "hot walker"
      (someone who walks alongside a horse
          holding a lead rope
              until it has cooled down &
              its coat has dried after workouts),

while Sirhan was seeking to be an "exercise boy,"
      one who actually rides the steed
              during exercising

—on his way to becoming a jockey.

So Sirhan telephoned an acquaintance named Frank Donnarauma
to see if he had a job for him. Donnarauma
said he had nothing

but the next night called Sirhan at home on Howard Street
                in Pasadena
& informed him there was a job opening
at the Granja Vista del Rio Ranch
owned by one Bert C. Altfillisch
                in Norco, California
                near Corona in Riverside County.

Donnarauma told Sirhan, yeah, he'd get a chance as an exercise boy,
so Sirhan went out there & was hired—
but first he had to work at everything associated with the horses.

Then Sirhan, known at the ranch as Sol,
led a protest of exercise boys.
Apparently, they were ready to strike—they wanted to exercise
colts in the morning, but nothing else in the afternoon
(such as grooming or stable work).

Sol/Sirhan delivered a speech after which Altfillisch
                refused to budge, saying if they didn't
                like their routines, they could leave.[17]

            A female coworker of Sirhan's
            at the Granja Vista del Rio Ranch
            later told the FBI that
                Sirhan "lived near the
corner of Fifth and Hamner in Norco, Calfornia.
She believes that he lived alone or with someone who
worked in the area. She said she was never at his residence
but had seen his car parked on that corner several times and
assumed that he lived right in that area.

"She said he did not like the Norco area and commented
that he had traveled home most of the time on weekends to
Pasadena and that he continually talked about how much better
Pasadena was than Norco."[18]

Wanted to be a jockey

An exercise boy named Edward Antwerp
lived with Sirhan at the Highlander Motel and another place
for about five months. Antwerp told the FBI

"About all he did at the motel was sit around quietly drinking
tea in great quantities. Sirhan went home
                    to Pasadena on weekends."[19]

Fall from a Horse
September 25, 1966

There was a heavy fog upon
the exercise track on a Sunday morn along the
                    bottomlands of the Santa Ana River.

Some owners had driven from LA to
view their quarter horses running

and were unhappy when the trainers
hesitated because of the fog.

There were a total of three steeds
ready to race
        in the fierceness of the fog.

(Sirhan, using jockey talk,
called it "breezing the filly.")[20]

            —page 71, File 1, Sirhan's Medical Records
            Philip Melanson, RFK archive, UMass Dartmouth

The contest began, & Sirhan's horse,
a chestnut mare named Hy-Vera
had maybe a half-length lead
when there was a foggy collision
and Sirhan was thrown down to the mud.

He lay there, semiconscious
crying out

Sol

until an ambulance arrived
and took him to Corona Community Hospital.

Dr. Richard A. Nelson was one of the doctors
and later told the FBI: "Sirhan questioned all of
the medical applications and all medicines administered
to him and appeared unduly frightened
of the various treatments.

He was one of the most reluctant patients
I ever had."

(Sirhan picked up his final check from Altfillisch
on December 6, 1966, his dreams of becoming
a jockey dashed.)[21]

The time track is somewhat confused,
but Sirhan apparently
was hospitalized overnight but signed himself out
the next day, and was back at work in a week

Then the next week, he again fell, reopening the eye-cut
so that he returned to the hospital.

"At first, Dr. Richard Nelson referred him to two
eye specialists working out of the same office in Corona,
Dr. Paul Nilsson and Dr. Milton Miller.

Sirhan complained he suffered pain, blurring,
and 'extreme motion' in his eyes, but they found no
evidence of an eye injury, and Miller thought Sirhan
was exaggerating."[22]

Millard Skeets Comforted
Sirhan after His Fall

Horse owner Millard Skeets
told the FBI
that after Sirhan and the others
raced off into the fog
for just a few seconds

A foggy collision

"he heard the horses squealing
and there was a crashing sound
                    and someone screamed."

        Skeets told the FBI "he ran down the track to a distance
        of about 3/16 mile
                and he found Sirhan lying in the dirt
                against a post on the railing.

        "At first he saw some blood in Sirhan's ear
        and suspected an internal injury; however, he saw later
        the blood came from facial cuts
                        and was merely running into his ear.

        "Within the space of about two minutes
        Sirhan was conscious and appeared frightened
        because he could not see due to the mud
                        and blood in his eyes.

        "He was bewildered and frightened, thinking he was blind."
        Mr. Skeets comforted Sirhan, holding his head
        in his lap, waiting for the ambulance.

        (The Corona Community Hospital
                admission form states
                        that this was the first visit to a doctor
                                        in Sirhan Sirhan's life.)

        Skeets told the FBI that Sirhan
                returned to the Granja Vista del Rio Ranch
        the second day after the accident
        & Sirhan thanked him
                for his help after the accident.[23]

        On the other hand, Sirhan's close friend, Terry Welch,
                told the FBI that Sirhan
                        was in the hospital for several weeks
                                        after the fall.

From Medical Records, Corona
Community Hospital
9-25-66 11:30 a.m.

"Problem: Fell from race horse, hit fence, sustained multiple injuries:

> Contusion of the left subscapular-dorsal area
> Laceration and hematoma of left upper lid
> Bilateral sand foreign bodies of the eyes
> Contusion of the left hand
> Lacerations of the chin-neck
> Multiple superficial abrasions.

"This 22 yr old Arabian male was riding a race horse when it veered toward the fence and he fell off, causing the above-described injuries. He was brought in by ambulance. Clothing was removed and the above-described injuries noted and treated.

> Eyes were irrigated with saline after 1/4% Pontocaine gtts.
> Neosporin ung.
> Chin laceration sutured
> Spine, hand, shoulder films reviewed by Dr. Deeb,
> most probably negative.

"Patient has never been to a doctor, no major previous injuries. No surgery, no major medical illness. Denies knowledge of TB or Cancer or diabetes.

"System review is totally negative.

"Background: has been in US for some years studying, apparently has finished college, but prefers riding horses, has aspirations to become a jockey.[24]

—page 45 of 100-page File 1, "Sirhan Medical,"
Philip Melanson, RFK archive, UMass Dartmouth

Sirhan's Friend Says Sirhan
Was Hospitalized for Two Weeks

A fellow worker at Granja Vista
was Terry Welch, who considered
Sirhan "his closest friend"
   during those months
   when both were exercise boys.

Welch told the FBI
Sirhan was in the hospital for a couple of weeks after the fall.

  Sirhan's head and back injuries resulted
  in Sirhan becoming partially blinded in his left eye.

"Welch advised that Sirhan underwent a complete personality change
after the above-described accident. He stated that prior to that time,
Sirhan had been good natured and easy to get along with. He was
popular with other employees at the horse farm.

  In Welch's view
  after the horse-fall Sirhan became a loner.

"Following his fall from the horse in 1966, Sirhan became a 'loner'
who was resentful toward anyone who had wealth. He, at this time,
became unpredictable and unreliable in that he would make plans to
do things or go places with Welch and then for no apparent reason
would change his mind."

  Welch told the FBI
  that after Sirhan was released from the hospital
  he got a job at another horse-trainer
  and stayed at this job for "3 to 5 weeks"
  then back to Granja Vista.

   As we have noted Sirhan's final check
   from Granja Vista was 12-6-66.[25]

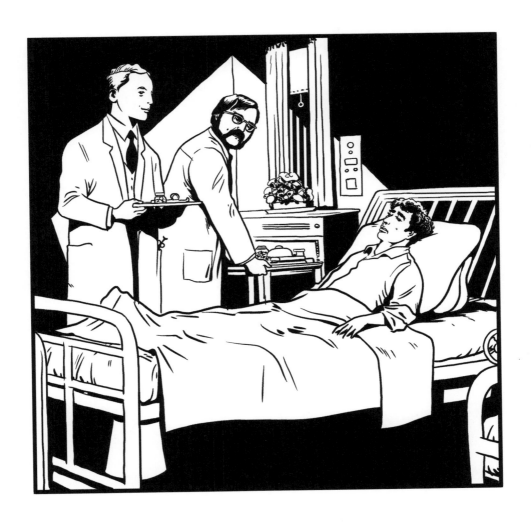

A prison-like hospital unit

Meeting a Strange Man "Who First Introduced the Idea That Government Officials Needed to Be Killed"

Beginning in 2008
     Sirhan was extensively interviewed and hypnotized
for 60 hours over a three-year period
by a Harvard University memory expert, Dr. Daniel Brown, in
association with an attorney named Laurie Dusek

     as part of an effort to gain a new trial for Sirhan.

Half of the interviews involved hypnosis,
and Dr. Brown reported, in a court filing in 2011,
that Sirhan Sirhan recalled that he
     was hospitalized for two weeks, out of the ken
of his family, after the 1966 horse fall.

It was then, as he recalled to Dr. Daniel Brown, that he was
kept in "a prison-like hospital unit."

After Sirhan Sirhan went "missing" for two weeks
after his accident
he came back "different" according
     to his family and friends.

Dr. Brown stated: "He remembers a 'prison-like'
     hospital unit
        where he drifted
in & out of consciousness, likely
under the influence of hallucinogenic
     & psychiatric drugs and hypnotic
        suggestions."

Likely It Was Then, in the Hospital, That He Was Isolated for Programming

Sirhan stated to Dr. Brown that he'd met
     "a strange man" with a foreign accent and
turned-down mustache, who, as described by Brown,

"first introduced the idea that government officials
needed to be killed; a memory of that same strange man sharing
a mutual interest in shortwave radios with (Sirhan Sirhan)."

(This mustached man later, in '68,
was seen at a police firing range with Sirhan.)

> Dr. Brown further reported in 2016
> that "Mr. Sirhan was an avid enthusiast
> of shortwave radios. He had a shortwave radio
> in his bedroom, and spent most nights
> before the assassination communicating
>   on his shortwave radio
>   with third parties.
>
> "Sirhan frequently entered a hypnotic state
> while communicating with other parties
> on the shortwave radio.
>
> "While in trance Mr. Sirhan would automatically
> write down what was communicated to him
> and subsequently was amnesiac for the content
>   of his automatic writing
>   in the spiral notebooks."[26]

FBI Chronology of Sirhan's "Medical Examinations"

In the FBI's document, "Chronology of Events—
Life of Sirhan Bishara Sirhan"
there are listings marked

> "Medical Examinations in connection with accident of
> falling from horse."

These occurred on
> September 28, 1966, October 26, 1966, November 8, 1966
> February 21, 1967, April 6, 1967, September 6, 1967

October 6, 1967, October 9, 1967
October 10, 1967, November 6, 1967
December 18, 1967

—some of them for robo?

RFK in Late 1966

At the close of '66, LBJ began
further intensive bombing
in North Vietnam.[27]

Rolling Thunder

1967

Intelligence Groups, Likely Also the National Security Agency, Surveilled Robert Kennedy
Early 1967

By 1967 he felt he could lead
        a great nation to a better,
        more peaceful time track,
    plus he hungered
      to bring to Justice those
        who had killed his brother.

In January of '67 RFK traveled to England, France, Germany & Italy
    where he was greeted with a great stir of approval.

    In London, he stayed with Lee Radziwill (Jackie
    Kennedy's sister) and her husband.

    January 26, he met with Prime Minister Harold Wilson
        at 10 Downing Street.[28]

In Rome, he saw Elizabeth Taylor and Richard Burton, who were filming
    Cleopatra

He had a 35-minute visit with the Pope, discussing the war in Vietnam.

    January 31, 1967,
        RFK called on President de Gaulle

      who told RFK, "There can be no peace
    in Vietnam until the United States
        stops the bombing of the North
        and announces its intentions to
            withdraw its troops."

      Withdrawal within a specific time,
      maybe even years.

     That same day, in the company of an American
     embassy official named John Dean
    RFK "called on Etienne Manac'h,
   director of Asian Affairs for the French Foreign Ministry.

Rome

Manac'h was in frequent contact with reps of
                    Hanoi & NLF (National Liberation Front).

He told RFK that Hanoi was ready to negotiate
with the US
                    provided that the bombing cease.

This "peace feeler"
                    subsequently appeared
                        in *Newsweek*

and LBJ assumed that RFK had leaked it.[29]

The "peace feeler" story caused headlines around the globe.

Johnson was angry. When Robert Kennedy returned to DC,
Johnson on February 6 asked him in at once for a meeting.

There was an angry confrontation at the White House.
RFK denied he had leaked the peace feeler to the media.

(*Time* magazine wrote a story on the argument.)

Kennedy told the angry LBJ
                    "I think the leak came from someone
                                in your State Department,"

        to which the angry one replied,
                    "It's not my department, God damn it,
                                it's your State Department."[30]

Walt Rostow and Nicholas Katzenbach, high LBJ aides, were in the room
                    during the Johnson-Kennedy tiff.

Johnson apparently threatened RFK along the following lines:

    "The blood of American boys will be on your hands.
I could attack you in exactly those words, and if I do,
                                        you will be finished."

RFK perhaps called LBJ an SOB at the February 6 meeting, and split.

LBJ apparently asked RFK to tell the press the US
        had never really received a peace feeler; RFK apparently
        did so, and that he'd never leaked any information.[31]

"The blood of American boys will be on your hands."

The National Security Agency

According to the *New York Times*
President Johnson received information about
Robert Kennedy's "personal activities and night life in Paris,"
probably from the National Security Agency.

In an article dated 10-12-75, titled "Spying on U.S.
Travelers Reported for 2 Presidents [Johnson and Nixon]"
by Nicholas Horrock,
the National Security Agency gave "private reports . . .
on what prominent Americans were doing and saying abroad,
apparently from electronic eavesdropping."

Did the NSA and other agencies
     keep on surveilling RFK
          after the trip to Paris
including during his upcoming 1968 presidential campaign?

And knew well what he was telling friends—
that he was going to get to the bottom
          of his brother's killing?

A JFK Investigation in New Orleans

On February 17, the *New Orleans States-Item*
ran an article that New Orleans District Attorney
          Jim Garrison
was investigating the JFK assassination.

One of the suspects was a man named David Ferrie,
whose body was found on February 22
     in his NOLA apartment.

There were questions about his death,
suicide notes were found,
     though he may have had a brain hemorrhage.

New Orleans Coroner Nicholas Chetta
conducted an autopsy
     and ultimately ruled that Ferrie
     had passed from natural causes.

A suspect dies in New Orleans.

Proving that RFK was following Garrison closely,
Kennedy called Coroner Chetta at home
to assure himself that Ferrie
had not been murdered.[32]

RFK on the Morality of the War

On March 2, 1967
Kennedy spoke to the United States Senate
describing his upsettedness on the war's morality

He spoke from the heart: "All we say and all we do
must be informed by our awareness
that this horror
is partly our responsibility;

not just a nation's responsibility, but yours and mine.

It is we who live in abundance and send our young men
out to die.
It is our chemicals that scorch the children
and our bombs that level the villages.

We are all participants. . . ."

The Senator proposed halting the bombing of North Vietnam
followed by an agreement "that neither side will substantially
increase the size of the war in South Vietnam
by infiltration or reinforcement."

And this: "Under the direction of the United Nations
and with an international presence gradually
replacing
American forces,
we should move toward a final settlement which allows
all major political elements in South Vietnam
to participate in the choice of leadership
and shape their future directions
as a people."

RFK had now
publically
broken
w/ the War Party.[33]

"But his glory is broken."

Phil Ochs Sings "Crucifixion" for RFK

The writer Jack Newfield, close friend of RFK, brought Phil to DC.
for Kennedy's speech. Newfield later told me:

> "In Washington,
>   March of '67
> Kennedy was giving his
> first full dress
>   speech against the war
> on the floor of the Senate.
>
> "It was a pretty good speech,
> and then afterward I took Phil into his office
> to introduce him to him, and Phil
>
>   ended up
>   singing, *a cappella,* with no
>   guitar
>
>   'Crucifixion'
>
> and Kennedy quickly grasped
>   that it was half about his brother—
> & it was a very heavy scene,
>   and he was wiped out by it"

—as Phil sang the final words:

And the night comes again to the circle studded sky
The stars settle slowly, in the loneliness they lie
'Till the universe explodes as a falling star is raised
Planets are paralyzed, mountains are amazed
But they all glow brighter from the brilliance of the blaze
With the speed of insanity, then he died—

> "A couple of times," Newfield continued,
> "later on he mentioned, 'How's Phil?'
>   and when Phil campaigned for
>   McCarthy, Kennedy said, 'Yeah, we'd like
>
>   to get him for us . . . That's
>   such a terrific song.'"[34]

Jim Garrison Announces an Arrest

On March 1, the day before Kennedy's speech to the Senate
New Orleans District Attorney Jim Garrison
    announced the arrest of 54-year-old Clay Shaw,
    formerly the head of the International Trade Mart,
    on charges of conspiring to kill John Kennedy.

    On March 17, a 3-judge-panel ordered
    Shaw to stand trial.

    Shaw would be acquitted in early '69,
        though it was pretty much successfully argued
        in books such as *Deadly Secrets* by Warren Hinckle
        & William Turner
            that Shaw had connections with Oswald

(And, at the time of Shaw's trial, CIA director Richard Helms
had ordered his top assistants to "do all we can to
help Shaw.")

        and that Shaw was associated with the CIA.

Not Until I Am President

Right around the time of Garrison's announcement
Look's editor in chief (since '66),
William Attwood

(who had been
JFK's "secret liaison with Castro"
        during JFK's final days),

    had dinner with
    novelist Chandler Brossard
    (then an editor for *Look*) and Jim Garrison
    at the New York Press Club
        in NYC.

They talked till 1 a.m.
Then right away, that very night, William Attwood called RFK
to say Jim Garrison was on to something
and that he intended
to "throw the weight" of *Look*
behind Garrison

& he wanted RFK to
          commit to opening the case.

Bobby replied
     he agreed JFK was a conspiracy

"but I can't do anything
until we get control of the White House."

After hanging up the phone
Attwood suffered a serious heart attack

took three months to recover
          & *Look* never waded into the case.[35]

A Ballet in the Waters of Destiny

          In a way
          it was an oblique ballet
          the brother was undertaking

          quietly daring
          —with a dash of accepting fate—

          to go ahead
          and confront them

          Maybe he thought it was the Teamsters
          or Organized Crime

          or his opponents in the vast & seething Agency

          Was he even aware of the names
          E. Howard Hunt or David Atlee Phillips?

          Or the CIA & Military's own robo-assassin
                    programs?

April 1967

Robert Kennedy began work on a 25,000-word manuscript on the
Cuban Missile Crisis in April '67, for the *New York Times Sunday Magazine*.

In October of '67 he notified the *Times*
          he didn't want it published

Jim Garrison indicts Clay Shaw.

because he felt that by then
it could be suggested

he was releasing it as part of a plan to run for the Presidency.

Debate on Whether to Run, or Not
Late 1967-early 1968

There were discussions among various aides and friends, for
and against it

and, ever whispering in the life-tracks of friends:
that they might shoot the Senator
just like JFK.

In the fall of '67
Fred Dutton, former assistant secretary of state
for JFK and later LBJ, and soon to be a major
worker for RFK's presidential campaign,
wrote RFK
he felt LBJ would not run for reelection:

"He will not want to
risk a major debacle
at the end of a 35-year
public career.

"After New Hampshire
will be a moment of truth for him.
He will make his announcement then
or wait until after the Republicans nominate."

A Gallup poll showed
RFK's lead over Johnson
among Democrats
was now 51 to 36

(but polls
can be washed aswirl
in the storms of events)[36]

October 8, '67
there was a high-level gathering

46

Attwood to RFK: Garrison is on to something

at the Regency Hotel
in NYC

—Edward Kennedy, Stephen Smith,
Fred Dutton, Kenneth O'Donnell,
Charles Daly, John Burns, William
vanden Heuvel, Richard Goodwin, Ivan
Nestingen, Tom Johnston, & Pierre Salinger—

in which urging RFK to run for VP was discussed,
but most believed
   he would decline
      if LBJ offered it.[37]

November 30, 1967
  Eugene McCarthy, senator from Minnesota,
    announced he would challenge LBJ
        for the nomination

    on the issue of the war.

December 10, '67
  Lunch: RFK and his brother
  with a small group of advisers

  (Goodwin, vanden Heuvel, Ted Sorensen,
  Fred Dutton, Arthur Schlesinger, Pierre Salinger).

  One line of thought: if RFK jumped in
  & won the primaries
  but was denied
   the Convention by the bosses

  he could then run in '72
  as a leader
    selected by the people
      —turned down by the bosses.

  Edward K. urged his brother to wait till '72.

  At a second meeting later in the day
  with a larger group

  it was agreed that RFK should delay,
  and fashion another analysis in January.[38]

48

McCarthy announces candidacy.

1968

By the end of January
RFK was very, very occupied
    on whether to jump in
        or not.[39]

During breakfast January 31
    with a group of reporters in DC
        for an off-the-record discussion

        he was asked
        about running

    & replied no
    he'd not be a candidate
    "under any conceivable circumstance."

    Reporters asked for the okay
    to run the statement
        & RFK said yes.

RFK's press secretary Frank Mankiewicz
managed to dilute the statement to
"under any foreseeable circumstances."

    Then came the Tet Offensive.[40]

The Tet Offensive
January 30

The National Liberation Front attacked the new 6-story white-hued
US embassy in Saigon.

They blammed a hole through the 9-foot-tall wall,
then 19 of them surged into the compound
    running toward the main building

    but a marine slammed and clamped shut the
    huge teakwood doors before the NLF

"What the hell is going on? I thought we were winning the war."

could shoot inside
and fly the

Viet Cong flag
upon the parapets.

Thus began the Tet Offensive,
described as the great turning point of the Vietnam debacle,
as the NLF attacked 90 towns & cities in South Vietnam.

The idea was to snuff out the regime
o' General Nguyen Cao Ky and General Nguyen Van Thieu.

The much-respected CBS newsman Walter Cronkite
remarked on air,
"What the hell is going on?
I thought we were winning the war."[41]

On March 2
the human named James Earl Ray
got his diploma
from the International Bartending School
and on the 5th
had the sharp tip of his nose
removed by a plastic surgeon

in LA.

I wonder if he was then
in the clutches of the agents of robo-wash
fixing him up to be one of those "three-month patsies"?[42]

Ray and Hypnotism

On 11-27-67
Ray had called Dr. Mark O. Freeman,

a "clinical psychologist."

Freeman's diary said a call came from "James Earl Ray,
who wanted to overcome his shyness, gain social confidence,
and learn self-hypnosis so he could relax, sleep and remember
things better."

Robo-patsy?

Ray saw Freeman that same afternoon.

Ray then visited Freeman five times,
the last time apparently December 14, 1967

(from Gerald Frank's *An American Death*)[43]

January 4, 1968
    Ray visited Rev. Xavier von Koss
    "director of the International Society of Hypnosis."

    von Koss recommended three books on hypno
    later found in Ray's luggage
        when he was apprehended in London.

William Turner's and Jonn Christian's *The Assassination of Robert F. Kennedy*,
page 228 mentioned that Ray was living in LA immediately prior
to MLK hit & "did consult with a hypnotist named Xavier von Koss."

    There is more on von Koss in Dick Russell's
    The Man Who Knew Too Much, page 678.

He writes that William Bradford Huie interviewed the Reverend
Xavier von Koss, who did not recall exactly how or why
Ray had telephoned him for
an appointment. Ray already had several books on hypno.

von Koss's number wasn't listed in the LA directory at the time.

    Another patsy wired up by the
            military-industrial-surrealists?

February 1
    It was brutal image time
    as a violent chump named Nguyen Ngoc Loan,
        chief of the South Vietnam police,

        executed a captive
        being walked along a Saigon street,

        his arm outstretched to the victim's head
        then blam!

The moment after the shot seen round the world

an image shown the world
by AP photographer Eddie Adams
& NBC TV

The same day
    in New Hampshire
        Richard Nixon began his
            search for the White House
            (though he never really found the place
                        where Lincoln lived).

General LeMay: Bobby Is Going to Be Assassinated
Early February '68

General Curtis LeMay
        had retired from the Air Force
        and was living Bel Air, LA.
The singer Eddie Fisher,
            in his autobiography (page 340)
wrote about visiting LeMay
not long before Bobby announced his run:

    "Toward the end of our visit," wrote Fisher,
    "I happened to mention that I was going to
    Bobby Kennedy's for his wife's telethon
        (in DC on February 11).

        'Bobby Kennedy?' LeMay said without expression.
        'He's going to be assassinated.'"

    LeMay that year
    went on to run as vp
    w/ George Wallace
        for the American Independent Party.[44]

RFK Deciding to Tell McCarthy He Was Running
March 7

RFK wanted to inform Eugene McCarthy
        he was going to run.

"Bobby Kennedy? He's going to be assassinated."

Richard Goodwin, who was assisting McCarthy at the time,
was prevailed upon to tell McC.

He delayed doing this until March 10,
two days before the primary.

McCarthy said, "Tell him to support me. I only want one term
as President. After that, he can take it over.

Goodwin replied, "You don't mean that."

McCarthy: "I do. I've thought about it.
The presidency should be a one-term office.
Then the power would be in the institution.
        It would not be so dependent upon the person."[45]

RFK Answers Hamill

Writer Pete Hamill had written RFK from Ireland
imploring him to run,

then March 8, RFK sent him a telegram:

HAVE TAKEN YOUR ADVICE.
AM IN TROUBLE. PLEASE
        CALL HOME

—see page 402 of Larry Tye's *Bobby Kennedy:*
    The Making of a Liberal Icon

(Hamill joined in, & was there three months later
                        in the fatal hotel kitchen,

        plus this: was this telegram intercepted
        by the NSA, and fed forth
                into the anti-RFK nexus?)

Praying with César Chávez
March 11

Robert Kennedy knelt in prayer with
                        César Chávez

58

Communion

in Delano, California
as Chávez was ending a 25-day fast
in the midst of his historic search
for fair pay & safe conditions for farm workers.

RFK told the great Chávez
he would run

and also told close friends,
but that he was going to wait till after the New Hampshire primary.

Back in the fall of '67
Senator Eugene McCarthy
came to Robert Kennedy
to say that he was running for President
on an antiwar ticket
if Kennedy was not.

Kennedy felt that Vietnam
was a national tragedy
but believed that a challenge to Johnson
would be political suicide.

There was a rush of support for McCarthy
They called it the Clean for Gene phenomenon
as 5,000 people, clean-shaven, eschewing beards
and fresh of breath
worked through New Hampshire
in the earliest Democratic primary. Phil Ochs
was among them,
singing all over the state.

On the 12th of March
Eugene McCarthy
running on the peace-in-Vietnam plank

stunned Johnson by getting
42.2 percent vs. 49.4 for war
in New Hampshire

& Nixon bested write-in candidate Nelson Rockefeller.

Broker

Robert Kennedy thought McCarthy
        was weak on the poor & down-trodden
and talked with his friends incessantly
             to the click of the wingéd primaries.
He knew, should he win, he might split the party
           and give it to Tricky,
plus no incumbent had lost a renomination
        since Chester Arthur to James Blaine in '84.

The basic fact was that,
    for all his brilliance
           McCarthy lacked the manic metabolism
                    required to win.
As I. F. Stone put it,
    "A certain cynicism and defeatism
    seem basic to the man."

Wednesday afternoon, March 13,
    18 RFK high-level supporters
        met in Steve Smith's apartment
            to discuss the elections.

        An hour of discussion passed
        when Edward Kennedy was handed a note
        saying RFK
           was meeting right then with McCarthy
           in Edward Kennedy's office.[46]

March 13
    RFK was on Walter Cronkite's national news show,
    and then after dinner
        Kennedy got on the phone with Democratic
              honchos around the country,

    one of whom was Mayor Richard Daley of Chicago,
    who urged him not to run

    "I still wish the President would change his policy,"
    said Daley. "You wouldn't feel this way."

    Daley told Bobby he'd call Lyndon right away
        about setting up a high-level commission
        on Vietnam
           to seek a wider road to peace

If Johnson would allow it
        then Kennedy would not run against him.

Shortly thereafter Daley called back,
according to the pro-Kennedy account,
and said that Johnson had told him,
"I'm all for this commission.
"I'm waiting for Sorensen to give me the names."

Daley suggested that Kennedy contact
the newly sworn Secretary of Defense, Clark Clifford,
                        to move it ahead.

March 14
        Kennedy and Sorensen met with Clifford
                        at the Pentagon at 11 a.m.
                to talk about who might sit on the commission

Clifford then met with Johnson at 4 p.m.,
                pitched the list & the concept,
                & Johnson said no.

Clifford Calls during Dinner
Johnson Says "No Commission"
March 14

That evening there was a dinner party, 3 tables of 12,
                        at Hickory Hill—
editors and publishers
        from the New York Press Association.

At RFK's table sat *Village Voice* writer Jack Newfield,
who "argued vigorously for legalization of marijuana
        and shocked the older guests by candidly admitting
        he smoked it himself with some frequency,"
                        in the words of
                        one of Ethel Kennedy's biographers.

        RFK overheard
        and wrote a note to Newfield.
        Maybe you can talk about something else
        or you might cost me the nom,
        and signed it Timothy Leary

63

Kennedy had offered to stay out of the race
if Johnson would name a "high-level bipartisan commission
to re-evaluate"
            what the US was doing in 'Nam.

            Kennedy had suggested members of the commission
            (with RFK one of them).

During the Hickory Hill dinner
Kennedy was called from the table
It was Secretary of Defense Clark Clifford
with the answer from Johnson.
No commission
            & Kennedy had to enter.[47]

My Lai
March 16

In a tiny fishing village called My Lai 4
Americans landed in helicopters
            and began four hours of the most hideous slaughter
            known to humanity.

There were rapes, disembowelments,
the burning of innocent thatched huts,
women forced to do blowjobs then slaughtered
mothers facing death protecting babies
            & people desperate
                        to slide beneath the already dead,

all in the name of American glory.

The 105 American troops were called Charlie Company;
they'd been in Vietnam for 3 months.
Finally, after the hours of evil,
400 old men, women, children lay killed,

and then a heroic helicopter pilot named
Hugh Thompson
            with crewmen Lawrence Colburn & Glenn Andreotta
            by chance in the air above

My Lai

landed while soldiers were still killing civilians
       in a ditch
and ordered the troops of Charlie Company
       to stand away.

Thompson had his support crew put guns on
the Americans, said he'd shoot them
    if they killed more Vietnamese

Then had his staff, in his own words,
      "wade in the ditch in gore up to their hips"

while he and his crew rescued about 11 Vietnamese
     from the butcher-batty young men.

   Thompson, now seen to be an American hero,
   was, back then, ostracized, threatened with a
   court-martial,
     and risked assassination from the
     Phoenix-wrecked climate of murder
      in the long thin land of hell.[48]

RFK Announces
March 16

In the Senate Caucus Room
    where his brother once declared,
Robert Francis Kennedy announced for President.

  (It was My Lai morn.)

Ethel was there with 9 of their kids.
Robert stood in a blue suit
    and a gold PT-109 tie clasp
reading his speech
    from a black notebook typed in overlarge letters

  He began, "I am announcing today
    my candidacy
     for the Presidency of the United States

"To close the gap between black and white,
rich and poor, young and old."

"I do not run for the Presidency
        merely to oppose any man
                but to propose new policies.

"I run because I am convinced
that this country
        is on a perilous course
        & because I have such strong feelings
        about what must be done. . . .

"I run to seek new policies—policies to close the gaps
between black and white, rich and poor, young and old
        in this country and around the world.

"I run for the presidency
        because I want the Democratic Party
        & the United States of America
                to stand for hope instead of despair,
                for reconciliation of men
                        instead of the growing risk of world war."

He said his decision "reflects no personal animosity or
        disrespect
                toward President Johnson."

He commended LBJ's serving JFK
"with the upmost loyalty. . . . I have often commended
his efforts in health, in education, and many other areas. . . .

He pointed out that "the issue is not personal. It is our profound
differences over where we are heading.

"I do not lightly dismiss the dangers
                        and difficulties
of challenging an incumbent President, but
these are not ordinary times
                & this is not an ordinary election.

"At stake is not simply the leadership
        of our party or even our country—it is our right
                to the moral leadership
                        on this planet."

St. Patrick's Day

And then he headed for
      NYC
         to march in the St. Patrick's Day parade.

Nixon Gazing at the Tube

Nixon watched Kennedy's speech
in a hotel in Portland, Oregon.

With him was one of his main henchies, John Ehrlichman.

Nix stared at the screen even after it was turned off,
then said, shaking his head,

"We've just seen some very terrible forces unleashed. Something
bad is going to come of this. God knows where this is
going to lead."

      Ask General LeMay.[49]

The Party Bosses
and the Big "Uh-Oh"

Just as big-city Democratic bosses (and others),
sensing Roosevelt's plummeting health,

axed Henry Wallace from the ticket in '44,

the Democratic "Party Bosses,"
such as Mayor Daley of Chicago,
            "controlled the nomination process."

High FBI Man Urges RFK Brain Spatter

The deputy director of the FBI, Clyde Tolson,
beneath the doursome J. Edgar Hoover,
responded to Kennedy's announcement
(according to writer Thurston Clarke):

"We've just seen some very terrible forces unleashed."

"I hope that someone shoots and kills the son of a bitch."

March 17, 1968
    Kennedy flew to Kansas City
         to begin his campaign.

  How would he be received
        was the question on his supporters' minds.

He'd chosen to give his first speech at KSU in Manhattan, Kansas.

    When his plane landed at the KC airport,
    he boarded the private plane
    of Kansas Gov. Robert Docking

    to fly to Topeka
    where there were over a thousand cheering supporters
         to greet him

March 18
    in Manhattan, Kansas,
         14,500 in the fieldhouse.
    He told them how
    a huge struggle was tormenting America
    not for who would rule
        but for the heart of the nation—
    in the campaign months
        Americans would have to make
        decisions on what the nation will stand for,
        what kind of citizens?

"If you will give me your help, if you will give me your hand,
      I will work for you
        and we will have a new America."

It was as if an explosion had occurred.
Students surged, shouted, beat chairs together
and pressed toward the candidate
      in a hot high-metabolism moil of Yes
till he finally got outside to stand in a convertible.

    Then, the same day, a second speech
    at KU's Allen Fieldhouse in Lawrence

with 19,000 on hand.

Flying in His Brother's Topcoat
March 18

RFK had been chilled riding in a convertible
and "huddled in his late brother's topcoat"
          on the flight back to Washington,

     talking about the faces of the students

     so expecting, so pent-up with
                    hunger for a differing American time track.

RFK Trip to California

Saturday, March 23, RFK flew from JFK to San Francisco—
during the flight
          the tired candidate plunked down
          pillows & blanket
               on the plane aisle
               for some shut-eye.

In SF then 2 Boeing 727
charter jets took them to Stockton, to Sacramento, San Jose,
          Salinas-Monterey & LA (on Sunday at the Greek Theater)
               during the next 1 1/2 days,
                    then on Monday, March 25
                    off to Oregon.

     Writer Jules Witcover in his book *85 Days*, wrote of:
     large and energized crowds
               "in an intensity and scope
                    that was awesome and frightening."

          —Jules Witcover, *85 Days*, page 113

     Huge huge huge
     upsetting no doubt

to those who would plot
an assassination in the kitchen.

March 24, a Sunday
RFK's Defenses Perhaps Tested by Robo-Washers

After landing in Los Angeles the afternoon of the 24th,
a huge crowd followed RFK through
a lengthy tunnel at the airport out to the street

and then on the way to the rally
bumper-to-bumper traffic w/
autos abandoned along the roadsides.

RFK spoke to 11,000 filling
& spilling beyond the Greek Theater in LA.

Nearing the close of his talk that day
RFK said, "The failure of national purpose
is not simply the result of bad policies
and lack of skill.
It flows from the fact that for almost the first time
the national leadership is
calling upon the darker impulses
of the American spirit—not, perhaps

deliberately, but through its action & the example
it sets—an example where integrity, truth, honor
and all the rest seems like words
to fill out speeches
rather than guiding beliefs."[50]

Those who robo-washed Sirhan
may have tested RFK's defenses at the Greek Theater:

The day before the rally, a young man named Steven Ahern
called the Greek Theater & announced,
"There is a bomb inside.
It will go off tomorrow afternoon at 4:30 p.m."

The first campaign trip flying to California

Ahern later told the FBI: "I knew prior to making this bomb
threat that the Senator was to address a rally at the Greek Theater
at 4:15 p.m. the
day after I made the telephone call.

"Later that same day (i.e. the day before Senator Kennedy
was to appear at the Greek Theater) at approximately 4:00 p.m.

I telephoned the *Los Angeles Times* and told
whoever answered the telephone that
'Senator Kennedy will be shot.'

"At approximately 1:00 p.m., I telephoned American Airlines
at Los Angeles International Airport and told whoever answered the
telephone, 'Senator Kennedy
will be shot when he lands.'

"This call to the airport was made from a public
phone booth on Laurel Canyon Blvd.

"Immediately after making the telephone call to the LA Airport
I drove to the airport and saw Senator Kennedy land and
was even able to shake his hand.

"After having seen the Senator at the airport, I drove to the
Greek Theater where I observed the entire Kennedy rally.

"I originally made the three calls involving the
aforementioned threats in order to
see what news that it would create."

Ahern told the FBI that on Monday, March 31,
he made an appointment with his psychiatrist
at Olive View Sanatorium, a Dr. Cagle.

(Olive View is located in San Fernando,
not far from LA.)

Ahern wanted "to explain that he had an urge to kill Senator Kennedy
for some reason which he was unable to explain within himself."

The FBI reported that Dr. Cagle, hearing of Ahern's
threats and his urge to kill RFK,

76

informed Ahern's probation officer,
                a man named Gottleib in Van Nuys,
"and Gottleib arranged to have Ahern's probation suspended
on May 3, 1968, in Division 20,
Municipal Department number 95, Superior Court,
LA County for a Sanity Hearing.

"Ahern was interviewed by two court-appointed psychiatrists
who declared Ahern legally sane on May 10, 1968." On May 15,
a Municipal Court judge sentenced Ahern to 3 years

"active probation under the supervision of Officer Gottleib on
condition that Ahern regularly see a psychiatrist."[51]

> —FBI report, 6-6-68, of Steven Dale Ahern
> in green 3-ring binder, #4-3A, RFK/FBI files
> pages 925–926, in bankers box in gray baby barn

Olive View Hospital/Sanatorium

Olive View Sanatorium was associated with UCLA. One of
Sirhan's doctors who treated him at Corona Community Hospital
in 1966, Dr. Richard Nelson, listed a "residency"
at Olive View Hospital in 1966.

Huge Reception in Los Angeles Drawing Attention of RFK Kill Team
March 24, 1968

Those who conspired to kill him no doubt
            took notice of the huge crowd in Los Angeles.

As Jack Newfield noted in his *Robert Kennedy: A Memoir*
                (page 241)

> "Later that night, Monday's *Los Angeles Times* hit
> the streets with the huge, eight-column,
>   two-deck headline:

> KENNEDY BESIEGED
> Senator Gets Wild LA Welcome

The lead story, by Carl Greenberg, began:

> "Senator Robert F. Kennedy was greeted here
> Sunday by one of the wildest demonstrations
> ever given a political figure in Los Angeles. . . .
> The reception Kennedy received here was
> uproarious, shrieking and frenzied."

At a Huge Rally at San Fernando Valley State College RFK Is Asked "Who Killed John Kennedy?"
March 25, 1968

RFK gave a speech to 12,000 listeners
at San Fernando Valley State College,

then said he'd take questions from the sea-tide crowd.

"Will you open the archives?!" someone shouted,
and others also shout-urged, "Open the archives."

A woman added, "Who killed John Kennedy?
We want to know!"

"Your manners overwhelm me," a startled RFK
said to the woman, but then he added,
"I haven't answered this question before.
But there would be nobody
that would be more interested in all
of these matters as to who was responsible
for the, ah, the death of President Kennedy
than I would."

As for opening the Warren Commission archives,
Kennedy said that he would, "at the appropriate time."

But, RFK also told the huge crowd
"I have seen all of the matters in the archives.
If I became president of the United States, I would not
reopen the Warren Commission Report.
I stand by the Warren Commission Report,"

Crowds in California

just the opposite of what
he was telling close colleagues
in private.[52]

—Bryan Bender and Neil Swidey, the *Boston Globe*,
June 1, 2016, "Robert F. Kennedy Saw Conspiracy in
JFK's Assassination."

Possible Place(s) Where Sirhan Was Worked On:

Olive View Sanitorium in San Fernando, Calif.
    connected with UCLA

Corona Community Hospital

California Rehabilitation Center in Norco/Corona, Calif.
    (near Naval Weapons Assessment Center)

A "clinic" mentioned by Candy Jones where she said
her CIA programmer Al Carsen "picked him up (Sirhan) at the clinic."

Sirhan Bishara Sirhan

In another part of the world
        the young man named Sirhan Bishara Sirhan
        had been driving a delivery truck
                    for an organic health food store
                    in Pasadena.

Sirhan had a dispute
with John Weidner, owner of the health store,
over a delivery schedule.
Sirhan quit on March 24.

Shortly thereafter, Sirhan demanded $300
severance pay.
        Weidner refused.
Sirhan wanted the matter before the
California labor commissioner.
        Weidner agreed.
On April 24, 1968

LA Labor Commissioner M. A. Myers
heard the case.[53]

According to an FBI interview with John Weidner,
"Weidner was required to pay Sirhan approximately
$150 for wages due and severance pay."[54]

On April 5, Sirhan received an insurance check for $1,705
related to his fall from the horse in '66
from the Argonaut Insurance Company.[55]

He cashed it, and placed $1,000
into the care of his mother Mary.

It appears that it was while in the hospital
after the fall
that Sirhan Sirhan
was first worked on
to prepare him to become a robo-killer.

He continued, after hospitalization,
to live with his mom in Pasadena
& dropped out of sight
for three months
beginning in late 1967

(according to a LAPD officer to
William Turner and Jonn Christian, cited on page 208
of their important book, *The Assassination of Robert F. Kennedy*).

It may have been then
they completed robo-washing him into a patsy
or a programmed assassin.

In *The Search for the Manchurian Candidate*, John Marks quoted an
unidentified CIA researcher, from the old days, who alleged it would be
much easier to make a "patsy" programmed to "make authorities think the
patsy committed a particular crime"
than to program a robot assassin.
Hypnosis expert Milton Kline, unpaid consultant to CIA researchers,
guessed to Marks he could
fashion a patsy
in a mere three months.

Sirhan was very, very easily hypnotized.

Johnson Abdicates
March 31

At the end of month
Johnson was telling people he would not
      win any of the upcoming primaries:
      Wisconsin, Indiana, Nebraska, Oregon, Calif.

and so on April Fool's eve
      Johnson abdicated
            in a television talk to the nation.

      He lifted the crow's feet that spread
      out from his eyes to his dangling ears
            in a goodbye smile.

         (After decade 'pon decade of study,
         I'm wondering if Johnson
            stepped away from rule

         because he was informed, or learned,
         that the military/intelligence/CIA complex
         had MLK in its rifle sights
            & RFK as well?)

      McCarthy was winding up his campaign in Wisconsin.
      Robert Kennedy was returning from his
            first campaign trip
      and was told when the plane landed
               at JFK
      with a large group of fans
            by the exit ramp.

Late that night Kennedy
     sent Johnson
     a telegram
        calling his no-run decision
            "truly magnanimous."
(Sorensen, Schlesinger, Walinsky, RFK and
others helped write it.)

April 2, 1968
  RFK
    visited LBJ
        at the WH

    where the President introduced him
                to his grandson, Lyn.

    RFK
    realized that
    the Pres would use his persuasion
    to prevent him from the nomination

    but no longer could fear
            after his abdication

    that RFK
            would bump him.

    They said goodbye for
    the last time. It was cordial.[56]

Martin Luther King and the Memphis Garbage Workers Strike

Down in Memphis
the garbage workers were
                treated like dirt
There were 1,300 of them, mostly black
—low-paying jobs, no job security, no insurance.
They hauled the garbage around in old leaky leather tubs
                on their shoulders
  and no place for shelter in the rain
  because white folk didn't want them on their porches.

The workers were members of
                the American Federation of State,
                County and Municipal Employees
  but the city refused to recognize them.

Two workers
got into the barrel of their truck,
a big cylinder with
             a built-in compactor,
        during a rain storm

and were crushed.

A few days after the crush
there was another rainy day.

the mostly white supervisors were permitted to wait in the barns
playing cards till the rain stopped
and were paid for the full day,

        but 22 black workers were told to go out and collect it
        in the rain
                 or not get paid.

        They went home
        and were paid two hours.
        So, on Lincoln's birthday, February 12
        they struck.

The same day that RFK thunder-voiced at Kansas State
        Martin King broke into plans
                        for the Poor People's March
        & came to Memphis
                 to speak to the strikers.

Mayor Loeb had replaced them with scabs.
There'd been a protest march,
police ran over a women's foot,
men rocked the car,
police then maced a number of ministers,
after which there were daily marches to city hall
                        & a boycott of downtown.

They asked King
             to come and help
as busy as he was with the March.

Memphis garbage workers strike

He spoke to a huge crowd
and said he would return
                    in a few days for a General Strike.

"I want a tremendous work stoppage,"
                              he told them.
"All of you, your families and children,
will join me & I will lead you on a march
                    through the center of Memphis."

The Poor People's March

The great Martin King at the time
was leading the plans
          for a March on Washington
                        for April 22,
which, had it been allowed to happen,
might have
      changed America
      for the permanent better
(which is perhaps
      why he wasn't allowed).

The March on Washington
              was much more truly revolutionary
              than scads of New Left dither.
It would have trembled America
      with its simple mode of
                  "jobs, income and a decent life."

3,000 poor people
blacks, Puerto Ricans, whites, Indians, Mexicans
would go by caravan to DC,
                    pitch tents and sleep in them
& each day delegations
          would go to government departments.

The numbers wd increase
                to great size.
They'd stay camped out
          till there were results from the gov't.

"I will lead you on a march through the center of Memphis."

Memphis Police Spy on King from a Firehouse as the Fates Begin to Spin and Measure
April 3

Martin King flew to Memphis from Atlanta
and checked into the black-owned Lorraine Motel
           where he often stayed.

(It appears that King had been scheduled to sleep
      in a room downstairs
           out of sight of snipers
                but had been moved to
                an easy target location
     based on a phone call the motel owner had received
urging that he be moved.)

Around noon a black detective named Redditt
went to a back room at a nearby fire station
and taped a newspaper to a window
        that looked out upon the 3rd-floor balcony
        of the Lorraine (King's room).

He cut out holes in the newspaper
        then put his binoculars up against them
in order to jot down the license plates
        and names of visitors
and, as much as possible,
      to note who did what.

The detective was joined by another black patrolman
        & between them they could identify
      virtually all the
           black activists in Memphis.

In the early evening of April 3, not long after 7,
    James Earl Ray
       in role as Eric S. Galt
          checked into the New Rebel Motel
              in Memphis.

Spying holes in a newspaper

A Thrum of Rain
evening April 3

A spring rain thrummed the metal roof
                    of the Masonic Temple
as 2,000 supporters wildly applauded
when Martin King came up the steps
                    for a glorious speech

at the end of which he spoke with the same tone of
acceptance
            as Malcolm X had
                    just before the Audubon Ballroom.

"And some began to talk about the threats that were out," said King
 "of what would happen to me
                from some of our sick white brothers. . . .
Well, I don't know what will happen now.
We've got some difficult days ahead.
But it really doesn't matter with me now.
                    Because I've been to the mountaintop!"

There was great applause, with thunder and lightning outside.

"And I don't mind. Like anybody I would like to live . . . a long life.
Longevity has its place. But I'm not concerned about that now. . . .
I just want to do God's will! And He's allowed me to go up to the
mountain. . . .
And I've looked over, and I've seen the Promised Land.
I may not get there with you, but I want you to know, tonight,
that we as a people will get to the Promised Land!
So, I'm happy tonight. I'm not worried about anything.
I'm not fearing any man!
    Mine eyes have seen the glory of the coming of the Lord!"

            —a speech truly to be listened
                & trembled to.

The Dire Day of Dream-Doom
April 4, 1968

The dire day of Dream-Doom
                whirls with hidden fury

90

"I've been to the mountaintop!"

years & years later,
for an evil that Evil wants kept in the cauldron
evil'd forth that bright spring Southern day

and just as Akhenaten's name
was chiseled out of
ancient Egypt's memory
so too modern power
has sought to erase what power
did to the great King.

After many years of studying the King case,
I have come to think that the books of William Pepper
have come the closest so far to tracing the truth
of what the military allowed to happen
& a racist power structure
despicably committed.

Army Officers Go to the Roof
of the Fire House the Day King Was Shot
morning, April 4

It was exactly a year since King spoke against the
war at Riverside Church.
"Somehow this madness must cease. . . ."

A man named Carthel Weeden was captain of the Fire Station #2,
located across the street from King's room 306
at the Lorraine Motel.
(The Fire Station was just down the same street as the rooming house
where James Earl Ray rented a room.)
Captain Weeden was on duty the previous morning
when two United States Army officers approached.
They said they needed a lookout for the Lorraine Motel.
They had briefcases, and indicated they had cameras.
Weeden escorted the military men to the fire-station roof
Where, behind a parapet wall, they had a bird's-eye
view of the open balcony in front
of Martin King's room

Military sets up shop.

(as well as a clear view of a brushy area where the actual
firing might have taken place).
Weeden left them there and returned to his duties.

On April 4
the 2 cameramen returned
and were in place
throughout the afternoon

including the fatal moment
at 6:01.

Army Security Agency Bugging the King Party at the Lorraine that Afternoon

Though Lenny Bruce's rule #16 (deny deny deny)
always is utilized
in order to scissor the past,
it is fairly certain that the ASA bugged 3 rooms
at the Lorraine that day
including Room 306,
King's room

& another room where a meeting with King went on
during the afternoon.

Pulling a Black Police Surveillor from Fire Station #2

Black Memphis Police Detective Edward Redditt
(in the 1990s a school teacher in Somerville, Tenn.)

at the time of April 4, '68
had been assigned to the intelligence bureau
and reported to a Lt. E. H. Arkin.

Redditt was sent with black patrolman
Willie Richmond of the intelligence bureau
to the locker room at the rear of fire station 2
on April 3–4

94

Bugged

where they could view the Lorraine Motel
from a window in a rear door.

As the day before, they cut holes
in paper placed over the window glass
in order to place binoculars up against them
to monitor the comings and goings
                    at the motel

On Dream-Doom Day Officer Richmond arrived
between 2 and 3—Redditt was already on duty.

Sometime after 4 p.m.
Lt. Arkin appeared and asked Redditt
to follow him to police headquarters.

He did, entering a conference room "where he said
he saw assembled twenty or more people, many of
whom he didn't recognize. Some were in
military uniforms,"
          as William Pepper describes on page 250
          of his book called *Orders to Kill.*

Chief Holloman told Redditt that a Secret Service
agent had flown in from Washington to tell
Holloman that a contract had been put out on
Redditt's life and therefore security would be provided
for Redditt and family.

Redditt protested, but Holloman ordered him home.
& just as Redditt came to his house
word came over the radio of the killing.

Ray Checks In to the Rooming House
3:15 p.m.

James Earl Ray, using the name of Willard,
          checked into a second-floor rooming house
                    above Jim's Bar and Grill
                    with a bathroom-window view
                              down the hall

96

Dream-Doom Day

(somewhat obstructed
                    by trees and foliage)
of Martin King's room at the Lorraine Motel.

(I wonder if the use of the name Willard
was not a twerpish mote of secret police satire
since Willard was the name of the hotel in DC
in which the FBI had acquired those
erotic tapes from early '64 they compulsively passed around.)

And then at 4 p.m., Ray drove to a gun shop
        in his white Mustang with Alabama plates
        to purchase some binoculars
                    (or somebody did).

        Law enforcement alleged that Ray
        crouched & leaned his 30.06
        on the sill till King
                paused on the balcony,

        but a later judge (who was an expert at rifles)
                pointed out that
                Ray's rifle was a pump-action
                and would have kicked back
                        if he had leaned the pump on the sill
                        as he fired,
                making it almost impossible
                        to hit his target as he
                stood, maybe with one foot in the bathtub
                            one foot on the floor
                    waiting for his brief moment
                    in history.

Pulling the Firemen

There were only 2 black firemen
at Fire Station #2.

That day they were pulled from duty there
                and sent to another station.

98

Checking in

Filming from the Firehouse Roof

From the roof of Fire House #2,
as Douglas Valentine wrote in
　　　　　　his book *The Phoenix Program* (page 338),
the military intelligence officers, perhaps
the very ones that Captain Carthel Weeden
conducted to the roof the previous day
　　　　　　and who had returned that Dream-Doom afternoon,
"reportedly watched and took photos
while King's assassin moved into position,
　　　　　　took aim, fired, and walked away."
William Pepper, author of three historic books on the
King assassination, uncovered a plan ordered by General
William Yarborough, assistant chief of staff
　　　　　　for Army Intelligence.

Under General Yarborough was an Army officer, who also
worked as a CIA officer; he was a Colonel

"William Yarborough was the man who gave him the orders
to organize the assassination of Martin King," said Pepper
　　　　　　at a lecture on his work on the King case.

The Colonel, said William Pepper
had previously been President Johnson's
briefer on the Vietnam War.

Why would the Colonel work on an assassination
　　　　　　of an American Civil Rights leader?

The Colonel's daughter told Pepper that the Colonel
"honestly believed that Martin King was a danger to the
security of the United States,
and he had no qualms about organizing that effort
because he believed that Martin King was a serious danger."

The Colonel, in Pepper's words, "coordinated the whole operation
from the 902nd Military Intelligence Group,
　　　　　　in the bowels of the Pentagon."

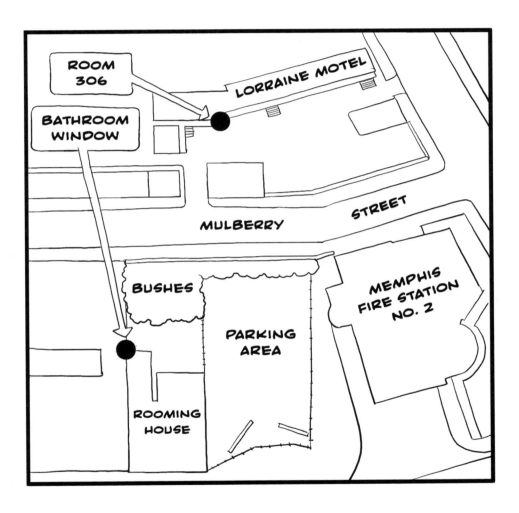

Line of sight obscured

On hand in Memphis that dire day
were two sniper teams, comprising, Pepper describes
 "an Alpha 184 unit, a unit that is normally a sniper unit."

Through a writer, Steve Tompkins, who had written a long
investigative piece on the role of Military Intelligence
infiltrating the Civil Rights movement,

Pepper arranged for Tompkins to
interview several of the snipers.

Pepper: "They laid out their presence in Memphis,
where they were, where the two guns were,
laid out that Andrew Young was also a target.

"Each sniper had a spotter" in their positions in Memphis.
"They were briefed at Camp Shelby at 4:30 in the
morning. (Shelby is in southern Mississippi, about a 5 hours' drive
                    from Memphis.)

"They were shown photos of King and Young, and these were
 the targets. These were enemies of the state. But they were told
'you are not to fire' until you're given orders by your captain."

The head of the team was on hand.

"They were there, in position.
        They described where
                Andy Young was,
                        and Martin on the balcony.

"And all of a sudden there was a shot.
                It hit Martin just above the jaw.

"One of the guys said they just thought the other team had shot first,
and they had got too anxious or something. But, it was very unlike
them,

"because they were so highly trained and disciplined.
        These were Special Forces guys.
        But the next order they received was to disengage.
        They disengaged and
                left the area the same way they came in."

Bushes at the bathroom window

King Is Murdered

King and Reverend Ralph Abernathy
were in a meeting in room 201
& then, at 5:40 went up the steps
                    to room 306.

Then, just before 6:00,
King came out onto the balcony

His associates were arrayed down below
& there was a limousine on loan from a
                        local black funeral home
            to take them to dinner.

He stood on the balcony
                for a minute or two
then back into his room.
Abernathy wanted to put on aftershave lotion.
King said he'd wait for him on the balcony
where he chatted with people
            including young Jesse Jackson of Chicago.

It was just at the moment
he was ready to walk down
                the iron-edged steps

        there was a single shot
                and King fell down
                        blood spurting from his jaw.

According to Ralph Abernathy's biography
And the Walls Came Tumbling Down (page 441)

"the black woman operating the motel switchboard
at the time of the shot
            . . . suffered a heart attack and died,
            thereby making outgoing calls impossible."

        —perhaps one should not rule out saxitoxin.

A single shot

Taking Pictures at 6:01

In William Pepper's book, *Orders to Kill,*
he writes (page 434) about interviewing one
of the two army photographers on the roof of
                              Fire House #2
across the street from the Lorraine.

At the moment of death
one photographer on the firehouse roof had
his camera trained on King on the balcony

& the other was filming and viewing arriving autos.

                    Bang!

The photographer filming King "said he was surprised
and in rapid succession quickly snapped four or five
photos following Dr. King as he fell to the balcony floor."

The other photographer, filming arriving autos previously,
"almost instinctively swung his camera from its parking
lot focus to the left and, focusing on the brush area,
caught the assassin (a white man), on film as he
was lowering his rifle. He then took several shots of him
as he was leaving the scene."

The two military photographers hand-delivered the pictures
to a Military Intelligence officer,
but the one who had filmed the shooter
kept the negatives and made another set of prints.

The sniper, Mr. Pepper was told, was not James Earl Ray.

The Actual Assassin

William Pepper describes it:

"Martin was killed by a civilian, firing from the bushes,
who was a sharpshooter, a Memphis police officer.
He was paid a sum of money to do it. He was the mechanic.
                    That's all he was.

The Mechanic

"He's alive, alive and well, and I've confronted him
in a non-threatening way, and I've asked him to talk to me. (He
agreed to meet but then didn't show up.) He took off, and he missed
a meeting, and I found out (from a contact) he went to visit his son,
in a small town in Virginia. His son works in this small town in
Virginia. I said, 'What's this small town in Virginia?'

The answer: "It's Langley, Virginia."
Pepper said that the shooter is "a very nasty piece of work,
        very dangerous guy, even at this age."

        A man named Loyd Jowers owned Jim's Bar and Grill,
        behind the brush area from which Martin was killed.
        After the fatal shot, the shooter handed the
                smoking gun to Jowers,
                        who broke it down.

        There was another Memphis policeman
        by the shooter
        who went down over the wall,
         ran up Mulberry Street, and was taken away
                                in a police vehicle.

        A taxi driver in the Lorraine Motel parking lot
        saw this guy come down over the wall
        from the brushy area where the shooter shot.
        The cab driver was killed that night,
        because he had seen
                something he shouldn't have seen.

The Thicket of Mulberry Bushes Cut

You know how young mulberry trees can grow
                                in bushlike profusion.
Photos taken at the hour of the murder show
there was a profusion of mulberry

by the edge of an 8-foot-tall retaining wall
                in back of
                        the rooming house

        where a shooter might have hidden himself.

Down go the mulberry bushes.

(The rooming house's backyard
was higher in elevation than the
street in front of the Lorraine Motel

& the retaining wall dropped down from
the backyard's higher elevation
                              to the street.)

By the next day the scrub brush that stood
        between the bathroom window
                      at the back of the rooming house
                      & the retaining wall

        presenting clear sight difficulties
                for someone leaning a pump-action 30.06
                on the sill of the window
                to focus on King on the balcony

                        had been cut away.

Branch in Front of the Bathroom Window

        Pepper interviewed an assistant to
        Fire and Police Commissioner Frank Holloman
        named Ed Atkinson,

        who recalled being at police headquarters
        after the assassination

        with 2 other officers

        one of whom said that he had been at the
        bathroom window in the boarding house's rear
        with 2 FBI agents.

        One of the FBI guys said that a tree branch
        would have to be cut

        lest no one would believe that
                an assassin could
                        make the shot.

Terrible news

[Many more details of this government murder
are to be found in William Pepper's excellent book of 2003
An Act of State: The Execution of Martin Luther King
and the 2016 *The Plot to Kill King: The Truth Behind the Assassination
of Martin Luther King Jr.*]

Robert Kennedy learned of the shooting just as he boarded a plane
on the way to a campaign stop in Indianapolis.

Robert Kennedy Recites from Agamemnon

His plane was in the air
with tentative word
and then it landed in Indianapolis
where he found out for certain.

He was making a campaign stop.
The Indiana primary was a few weeks ahead.

He drove to the rally,
about a 1,000 supporters
who hadn't yet heard the news.

RFK then delivered a spontaneous encomium
in praise of Martin Luther King
to a stunned audience

which included these lines::

"My favorite poet was Aeschylus.
He wrote
        'In our sleep
        pain
        which cannot forget
                        falls
        drop by drop upon the heart
        until
         in our own despair,
                        against our will,

        comes wisdom
        through the awful grace of God.'"

"Pain which cannot forget falls drop by drop upon the heart."

He'd first read those words
a few months after Dallas
when Jacqueline Kennedy had shown him Edith Hamilton's
                                    The Greek Way.

He read it carefully, also Hamilton's *Three Greek Plays.*

Did King's death alert Robert Kennedy to the danger
out there in the gun-batty darkness?
Or did it make him more quietly fatalistic
in the walled words of Greece.

In the ancient text of Aeschylus
        a chorus of elderly men by the palace
fills in the audience
            on the Trojan wars
                & the karmic knots & curse-based calamities
                        that were soon to befall Agamemnon
                        and the Trojan princess Cassandra,
                                whose boat was about to dock
        at the end of the long bay near Argos on the Peloponnesus.

The chorus approaches Klytemnestra
to learn about the news,
                given by a signal-fire
                        that Troy had fallen.

In the original Greek
the lines that Kennedy spoke
are mainly delivered in cretics
                        and iambics,
plus one example of the meter known as
the dochmiac, used for times of high emotion
& a spondee!———

    The Greek is very, very difficult

    Ahh, Robert Kennedy!
            what a thorny cluster of lines
            the bard has made
            his Argive elders chant!

I decided to translate a larger section of the chorus
beginning a few lines before the
            ones Kennedy chanted that stunned afternoon

A wisdom of the All

              to try to understand:

Oh Zeus! whoever he is!
(if this to him is a pleasing
name to be called)

This is how I name him
and I am unable to come up with any other
when I ponder it fully
except Zeus, and so it's meet to
hurl this follyful idea
              out of my mind.

Whoever once was great
teeming with war-hunger
shall not be said to have ever been alive,
while he that later grew
as a conqueror of land
              has come and gone

But someone who sound-mindedly shouts
victory chants to Zeus,
he shall build a wisdom of the All—

for Zeus, by leading mortals to
think things over
sets them on a useful path:

knowledge comes from suffering
in magisterial mightiness!

It drip drip drips in sleep
in front of the heart

—the relentless memory-pain—

so that even against our will
a wisdom of soul comes upon us!

thanks to the violent grace
of our divinities
              in their sacred throne-place of rule

      —lines 160-183

Riots

Be careful, o Robert Kennedy
Please do not venture forth
with the soul-searing knowledge of Aeschylus
making you heedless of the fatal anger

Anger, Grief, Riots

Anger and grief
  and a solid plutonian wall of injustice
      from the Earth to the Moon

   caused big riots in over 125 cities
      nationwide

  —Chicago, Baltimore, DC, Detroit, Boston—

  55,000 troops were sent to quell them.

  A flare o' fire
  as in DC where

  bayonet-affixed troops
  surrounded the Capitol.

"Guns Between Me and the White House"

  In DC, April 7,
  after the burning and destruction,
  he toured the devastation with Ethel.

Reverend Walter Fauntroy of the New Bethel Baptist Church
    in Washington, DC,
had a moment alone with RFK
when he asked him how the campaign was going.

Kennedy replied, well, and if he could win Indiana and Nebraska,
then it would build and he could win Oregon,
and if he won California,
    then he felt he'd get the nomination.

The FBI alerts campaign to "potential assassins."

He paused, then said,
    "But there's one problem."

"What's that, Bobby?" asked the Reverend.

"I'm afraid there are guns between me and the White House."[57]

> The FBI gave Frank Mankiewicz photographs
> of "potential assassins" every week.
>
> Mankiewicz would study faces at rallies
> and even at airports,
>
> trying to identify possible killers.[58]

(Mankiewicz was the son of the screenwriter for
Orson Welles' *Citizen Kane*. He had served in the Peace Corps
and had met Robert Kennedy when the Senator had made
a trip to Panama in 1965; then had signed on as a press aide.
By '68, Mankiewicz was the candidate's press secretary.)

RFK's Eye-Opening and Soul-Opening Trip to the Mississippi Delta
April 9–11, 1967

In March, RFK had learned with alarm
about hunger in the Mississippi Delta at a Senate hearing,

so on April 9, just two days after he had told the Rev. Fauntroy
there were "guns between me and the White House,"
along with other senators, Civil Rights activists
such as Marian Edelman plus a bunch of reporters & TV cameras,
            Kennedy flew into Jackson, Miss.,
                where among his greeters
                    was a gaggle of KKK-ers
                    shouting racist slogans & a sign:
            "let lbj send rfk to hanoi, not mississippi"

        The next day RFK and Senator Joe Clark
        drove into the impoverished Delta
                to see for themselves.

Mississippi Delta

RFK was moved to tears at seeing the hunger of children
in near-foodless shacks.

In one of them
        there was a photo of JFK on the wall
        but no running water, toilet or electricity.

Back in DC, RFK confronted the Agriculture Secretary
and convinced him to loosen the Food Stamp Rules
so that people with no income
        such as some he encountered
                would not have to pay the $2-a-month fee,

plus got a nonprofit foundation to
        dispatch doctors to examine 100s of children
        like the ones with illnesses
                he had observed on his visit.

And CBS, as a result of RFK's example,
produced a documentary called *Hunger in America*.

        (See Larry Tye's remarkable book, *Bobby Kennedy:
        The Making of a Liberal Icon*.)

The Daunting Flow of Primaries RFK Faced
May–June 1968

After his announcement in mid-March,
he entered the first primaries it was possible to enter:

(He missed the March 12 primary in New Hampshire,
        & April 2 in Wisconsin.)

        May 7, Indiana and District of Columbia
        May 14, Nebraska
        May 28, Oregon
        June 4, California and South Dakota

Coming up was the June 18 New York primary
        & other struggles
                to convince party powers.

(Just 14 states held primaries in 1968:
New Hampshire, Wisconsin, Indiana, District of C, Nebraska,
Oregon, California and South D,
Ohio, Pennsylvania, New Jersey, New York
Massachusetts and Florida.)

The Packed RFK Motorcades

Kennedy's motorcades
from black to ethnic neighborhoods
hands outstretched
blacks, whites
reaching

were a marvel
of the healing of divisions:

As Jules Witcover wrote about Kennedy in Indiana
in his book *85 Days* (try page 176):

"The neighborhoods ran smack against one another and you
could read their racial or ethnic composition in the faces that
looked up at him, in the color of the hands that stretched out
to him, in the accents that shouted at him, in the names on
simple storefronts."

RFK's security would hide the autos at night
after the motorcades
to prevent creeps from wiring bombs.

Delegate Situation

In late April
vice president Hubert Humphrey
announced for the presidency.

He was too late for some of the primaries
and decided not to run in the rest,

though he had surrogates run for him
(such as Senator Stephen Young in Ohio; Senator George Smathers
in Florida; and Governor Roger Branigan in Indiana).

He worked to pick up delegates in the non-primary states
Some viewed him as the front-runner.

RFK bested Branigan and McCarthy in the Indiana primary, and then
defeated McCarthy in the Nebraska primary.

After RFK's loss in Oregon, the California primary was vital,
to both Kennedy and McCarthy.

McCarthy appeared at California's numerous colleges and universities,
where he was treated as a hero for being the first candidate
in opposition to the war.

While RFK appeared in the larger cities in the ghettos and barrios,
where he was overwhelmingly supported

On May 7
RFK won his first primary, in Indiana.

The Yippies in New York,
eager for confrontation at the Democratic Convention,
I remember were glum that Kennedy was able to reach out to the
people
in ways that war-painted dope-jousters
                                    could not,
and so
        the plan, instead of a huge Festival of Life
        involving hundreds of thousands of protesters,
                evolved to take a few
                        psychedelic buses
                        on a cross-country tour to
                                the Democratic Convention
                                                in Chi

Liking Robert Kennedy

I liked Robert Kennedy
        I was hungering for his Presidency.

On the stump

Jack Newfield once told me
RFK frowned at cursing by his staff.
I thought, as I jotted at the time:
"better a liberal puritan
          who wouldn't use poverty as a tool
than a dirty-mouthed part-fascist populist."

Sirhan Goes to Topless Bar with Known "Communist" (& FBI informant)
May 2, 1968

FBI informant
      Walter Crowe
& a member of the Communist Party
called Sirhan Sirhan
      (at the urging of the FBI, a gov't agency?)
to arrange a meeting,

which occurred on May 2.

Sirhan picked up Crowe
      & drove to Bob's Restaurant
      on Colorado Boulevard in Pasadena
                    for coffee,

where they were joined by two friends of Sirhan.

Crowe then went with Sirhan
& Sirhan's acquaintances
            to a topless bar, the Highlife,
            where they drank
                  a couple of pitchers
                            of beer.

A FBI report states: "While at the Highlife,
which is a topless bar, the conversation generally
                  concerned girls and race horses. . . .
Politics were not discussed, and the name of
the late Senator Robert Kennedy was not mentioned."[59]

The Highlife

(I interviewed LA television producer Peter Noyes
                on August 8, 1975 in Los Angeles,
and asked how he'd learned Walter Crowe
was an FBI informant. He said it was FBI agent Roger
LaJeunesse who had told him. Robert Houghton's book on
the history of SUS was in the galleys stage. The FBI had
obtained a look at the galleys, and noted that
Houghton had dumped on Crowe as a possible perp, or
conspirator. They surmised that Houghton probably did not
know Crowe was an FBI informant. The FBI called Walter
Crowe and asked him if he wanted them to hip Houghton
he was a Bureau informant.

Crowe said no.

A Report by INS Investigator That Sirhan Attended Party at the Home of Sharon Tate

The Immigration and Naturalization Service (INS) was
an agency of the US Department of Justice from 1933 to 2003.
There was an INS investigator, Richard Smith,
who researched and prepared a report (in 1974) which stated
that members of an English satanist cult invited Sirhan Sirhan
to a number of parties that were sponsored by "television people"
in the LA area, and that one of the parties took place
at Sharon Tate's residence. At these parties, it was averred,
sexual and ritualistic rites were reported to have occurred.
In Smith's report, it was written that Sirhan Sirhan "had attended
some parties given by television personalities in behalf on the
organization, where rites took place usually dealing with
sexual deviations and heavy drug use. One of these parties took
place at Sharon Tate's home."

Such a party involving Sirhan had to have occurred in early 1968
or possibly late '67.

> (Sharon Tate lived in 1967 and early 1968
> at a house at 1038 Palisades Beach Road
> overlooking Santa Monica Beach, then by early 1968
> lived in a 4th floor apartment at the Chateau Marmont
> Hotel at 8221 Sunset Boulevard.)

MK-Ultra

A copy of Richard Smith's memorandum of 1974
is in the author's RFK archive.

Robo by May

If we accept the paradigm
of it taking the CIA robo-washers
a few months to program
a killer,

then Sirhan was likely a robo-killer by May.

I think that the intelligence agency robot-makers
had public interfaces,
probably some hypnotists in California
(and maybe a cult or two),

recruited killers,
did background checks
and did their work on them
preparing them to kill.

I think Sirhan would have
been isolated, checked out,
prepared for programming, programmed
then tested
to see if he would in fact
carry out a killing.

Robowashing, serial murder, napalm, Agent Orange
what a century!

Did CIA Director Richard Helms
Know of Sirhan's Programming?

The Director of the CIA, Richard Helms,
an avid proponent/supporter of Robowash research
was fired by Richard Nixon
in early 1973 & promptly ordered
all 20-odd years of CIA Brainwashing, Hypnotic Programming,

Candy Jones

Research into Programmed Assassinations, et al.
                totally destroyed,

so that actual records, say for brainwashing programs
at prisons & institutions in California,
                        are fairly scant.

The CIA and the military had developed the techniques
to fashion robe-assassins
                back in the 1950s.

Techniques are techniques,
and they existed in the spring of 1968.

There were those in the Los Angeles area in 1968
with government expertise in programming people
                    to be unwitting CIA couriers, at least.

Did one or more of them robo Sirhan's behavior
by programming him
                to shoot the candidate?

It's likely they started studying RFK's final 85 days,
parsing the campaign plans
till he could be isolated correctly
                & the scythe of the right
                            could cut

(a good book to read, which explores the question of robo, is
William Turner's and Jonn Christian's
                The Assassination of Robert F. Kennedy).

Candy Jones & Robo

Speaking of sleazesome robo-mumbles
such as Sirhan may have muttered over shortwave radio
upon the urging of his programmer(s),
the record of history is clear
that the CIA worked long & hard
to develop techniques of mind control
& even to create what could be termed

hypno-robotic killers
w/ very bad memories.

A good amount of mind-control research
was conducted in California—

Take the case of the one-time supermodel Candy Jones
who, as believably traced in the 1976 book by Donald Bain
The Control of Candy Jones,
worked twelve years ('60–'72) as an
unwitting
courier for the CIA.

Her programmer was a doctor in California
(reported to be a Dr. Albert Carsen, with offices in San Jose—
he was a obstetrician and gynecologist),

who created within her an alternative personality
which was summoned forth by means of
the good Doctor speaking
hypno-phrases
sometimes by telephone.

The courier work was done by the alternate personality.

(Donald Bain told researcher Martin Lee, during an interview in
April of 1978, that Candy Jones under hypnosis
stated twice that Dr. Albert Carsen had bragged about
hypnotizing Sirhan Sirhan.)[60]

Candy Jones Recalls Albert Carsen Alleging That He Had Hypnotized Sirhan Sirhan and Had Picked Up Sirhan at the "Clinic"

Candy Jones, in a hypnosis session with her husband John Nebel,
who had taken on the role of hypnotist Albert Carsen,
programmer of Jones—

Jones to Nebel/Carsen: "You said you first picked him [Sirhan] up at
the clinic.
You said he was so disoriented he was hysterical; he was a hysteric.

You met him at the clinic, you said.
You said that he was a very upset young man, very disturbed."[61]

—Tape #43, "Candy Jones," Box 8, Audiocassette
Records, Philip Melanson: RFK archive, UMass
Dartmouth

The Hypnotist Who Spoke Like Otto Preminger

JOHN NEBEL, IN ROLE AS DR. ALBERT CARSEN: Do you remember the
German doctor? Did I mention to you that he used hypnosis?

CJ (UNDER HYPNOSIS HERSELF): He wasn't German.

NEBEL/CARSEN: He wasn't? What was he?

CJ: He was from Vienna.

NEBEL/CARSEN: I always think that is the same as German.

CJ: Don't you remember? He made a big to-do about (garbled)
I called him an Erich von Stroheim, and he didn't think it was funny.

(Jones also said that the doctor sounded like Otto Preminger.)

Jones described later running into him at the Fairmont Hotel
in San Francisco in early June 1968

He was with RFK bodyguard, pro-footballer Roosevelt Grier,
in the lounge of the Fairmont.

Jones alleged that Grier knew the Viennese-accented doctor/hypnotist.

Grier also drove Ethel Kennedy that day to a television studio.
It was likely the morning of Sunday, June 2
when RFK (and Ethel) went to a television station for an interview,

then RFK and Ethel
           went to mass at a church just down the street
           from the Fairmont Hotel on Nob Hill.[62]

The hypnotist creates an alternate personality.

—Tape #43, "Candy Jones," Box 8, Audiocassette
Records, Philip Melanson: RFK archive, UMass
Dartmouth

May '68, Just Before RFK Hit, Godfather
of Hypno-Robowash William Estabrooks Reveals
Secrets in Newspaper Interview

William Estabrooks, head of the psychology dept at Colgate U,
was a visiting professor at Rhode Island College in 1968
and gave an interview to the *Providence Evening Bulletin*
                published May 13, 1968
under the headline "Visiting Prof at RIC Links Hypnotism
                with Assassinations and Espionage Acts."

In the interview Estabrooks commented on the use
                of hypnosis
                to operate robot espionage agents:
"This is not science fiction. I have done it."

The article states: "Dr. Estabrooks said that the key to creating
        an effective spy or assassin rests in
                        splitting a man's personality
                        or creating a multiple personality,
                        with the aid of hypnosis."

As ace RFK researcher Philip Melanson noted,
"Estabrooks was not a fringe player in the CIA's search
for the programmed assassin: he was one (if not the)
intellectual godfather of the idea."[63]

—Philip H. Melanson, February 1992,
"The Programming of Sirhan Sirhan: Some
Additional Data." Melanson RFK archive, Box 4,
File 20, UMass Dartmouth

Jones at a CIA-Funded Institute in Carmel

The book on Candy Jones reveals that on June 3, 1968
Candy Jones was brought to a CIA-funded institute

in California for a seminar
        conducted by another CIA robo-official.

(The institute was located in Carmel, California.)

This robo-doctor was ID'ed as famed doctor-hypnotist William
Kroger.

Kroger, long associated with the espionage establishment, had written
the following in 1963: "a good subject can be hypnotized to deliver
secret information. The memory of this message could be covered
by an artificially-induced amnesia. In the event that he should be
captured, he naturally could not remember that he had ever been
given the message. . . . However, since he had been given a
post-hypnotic suggestion, the message would be subject to recall
through a specific cue."
—William Kroger, *Clinical and Experimental Hypnosis*
        (Philadelphia: Lippincott, 1963), page 299

One question that awaits further releases
of CIA/California robo-research history

is whether Sirhan Sirhan
        came into their clutches
                & maybe even James Earl Ray himself
        (when he was in Los Angeles
        in early '68).

        Too weird?
        Nothing is too weird for 1968.

Did William Joseph Bryan, Jr.
Program Sirhan Sirhan?

Another possible Sirhan robo-programmer
was hefty 300-pound Dr. William Joseph Bryan, Jr.,
who had an office on the Sunset Strip

and claimed to have been in "the brainwashing section" of the US Air Force
        during the Korean War,

& "reportedly became a CIA consultant in its mind-control and behavior
         modification experiments."

During the Sirhan era, Dr. Bryan had set up a medical and hypnotherapy
business on the Sunset Strip
         called the American Institute of Hypnosis.

He was also involved in the "fundamentalist church circuit" in Southern
         California, "where he delivered fire-and-brimstone sermons."

         See, p. xxviii, Introduction, to *The Assassination of
         Robert F. Kennedy*, by William Turner and Jonn Christian

Dr. Herbert Spiegel told Christian and Turner that whatever is mentioned
under hypnosis in the presence of a hypnotized subject
         is retained permanently in his mind
         "especially if it comes from the hypnotist,
         and it might flow out at any time."

This caused the two to reexamine Sirhan's notebooks.

"Could he (Sirhan) have scrawled something during a trance regression
that the hypnotist had mentioned while programming him?"

They found a passage: "God help me. . . . please help me. Salvo Di Di Salvo
Die S Salvo."

This apparently referred to the Boston Strangler, Albert DiSalvo,
whom Bryan had hypnotized and from whom had elicited a confession.

(In 1969, the California Board of Medical Examiners deemed him guilty
of unprofessional conduct for sexually molesting four women patients
         who submitted under hypnosis.[64])

         Bryan died in a Las Vegas motel room in the spring of 1977,
         of natural causes, according to a coroner.

         Turner and Christian not long thereafter interviewed two
         Beverly Hills call girls
                  "who claimed to know Bryan intimately."
         These two had been "servicing" Bryan around two times a week
         for the last four years, usually together.

William J. Bryan, Jr.

For the last year of earthly life, Bryan had been depressed
and "the girls said to relieve Bryan's
depression they repeatedly titillated his enormous ego
by getting him to 'talk about
all the famous people you've hypnotized.'"

Bryan spoke about Albert DiSalvo, but then bragged
that he had hypnotized
Sirhan Sirhan.

"The girls didn't sense anything unusual in the Sirhan angle, for Bryan
had told them many times that he 'worked with the LAPD'
on murder cases, and they didn't know that he had absolutely no contact
with Sirhan following the assassination.
Both girls were certain of the name Sirhan Sirhan."

The ladies of the sex trade linked Bryan to the CIA.
He instructed them, at the beginning of their relationship with him,
to call an unlisted number at his office.
If someone besides Bryan answered, they were to announce
they were from
"The Company."

The women alleged that Bryan repeatedly stated he was a CIA agent but
also enmeshed in "top secret projects."[65]

Sirhan Sirhan Trance Writing
or Robo Writing While Talking Over
Shortwave Radio

During the long series of examinations by Harvard's
Dr. Daniel Brown in the 2000s,
Sirhan stated he'd met "a strange man" with a foreign accent and
turned-down mustache, who, as described by Brown,
"first introduced the idea that government officials
needed to be killed; a memory of that same strange man sharing
a mutual interest in shortwave radios with (Sirhan Sirhan)."
Brown noted that Sirhan's "passionate hobby as a shortwave radio operator
was never explored at trial."
Sirhan also had "a memory of learning to shoot at vital organs and human
targets with a 'range master' at Corona Police Firing Range," and that

Sirhan "signed in the Saturday before the assassination accompanied by a man fitting the description of the strange man with the turned down mustache and foreign accent, who refused to sign in."

And this, a memory of Sirhan that he "often wrote in his spiral notebooks
at night in an hypnotic state, while communicating with
other parties on his shortwave radio."[66]

Another statement by Dr. Brown:
Sirhan Sirhan "also specifically recalled
being given suggestions by an anonymous
party over his shortwave set
that he wrote down in his spiral notebooks
as suggested while in a hypnotic
state and while engaging in
automatic writing."[67]

Maybe William Bryan
was the person
who chanted
to Sirhan
over shortwave radio
& thus assisted in the writing of his notebooks.

A Sleazesome Robo-Diary
May 18

The 9:45 a.m. entry in Sirhan Sirhan's diary
shuddered the era:

"My determination to eliminate R.F.K. is becoming more the more of an unshakable obsession port wine port wine port wine R.F.K. must die--

RFK must be killed Robert F. Kennedy must be assassinated R.F.K. must be
assassinated R. F. K must be assassinated R.F.K. must be assassinated...."
    —and repeated nine more times before the grim words:
    "Robert F. Kennedy must be assassinated before 5 June '68. . . ."

Although it appears to me that the words 5 June '68
were written in a different handwriting

141

and that the pages of this diary
might have been written during robo-mumble.

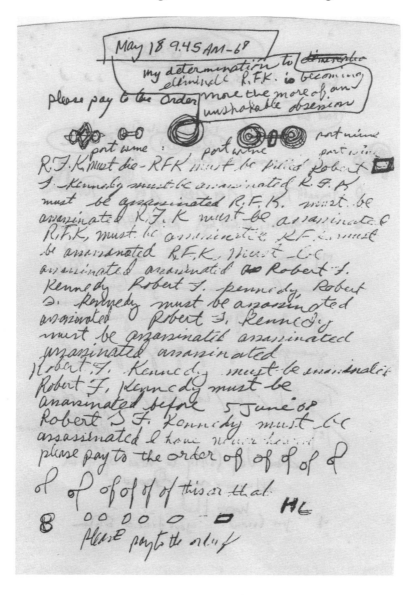

This well-known May 18 RFK-must-die page was written two days before
Sirhan Sirhan could have learned about RFK's support of Israel,
on a television program dated 5-20.

It has been pointed out that Sirhan Sirhan LATER blamed the
broadcast for

Radio-Robo

rousing his ire against RFK, though the May 18 entry
was two days before the broadcast.

Thursday, May 16, 1968
Meanwhile that day RFK flew between LA and Sacramento
campaigning fiercely.[68]

Day Off for RFK
Sunday, May 19

"Kennedy took Sunday off, a rare thing for him,
at John (& Evans) Frankenheimer's beach house
in Malibu. But Frankenheimer kept a flow of his own
social friends moving through, and Kennedy finally sought
refuge in a restaurant down the coast with Goodwin"[69]

Romain Gary Warns RFK about
Possible Impending Hit
Sunday, May 19

Pierre Salinger wrote in his book P.S. about how RFK wanted
a place for some rest:

"In late May he'd called me and asked me to find a place
where he could take a day off. I got in touch with the
Frankenheimers, who graciously offered to move into town
for a few days so that Bob and Ethel could have their
beautiful Malibu beach house to themselves.

"Then, Bob called again and said, 'Why don't you put together a
kind of a fun lunch on Sunday. Try to get some people out there
who will be a little different."

Salinger complied: Shirley MacLaine and Warren Beatty (her brother),
Angie Dickinson and Burt Bacharach, the astronaut John Glenn and
his wife Anne, John and Evans Frankenheimer, and actress Jean Seberg and
her husband Romain Gary.

Rfc K_lafspgl A_lbgb_rc

"You know, don't you, that somebody's going to
try to kill you?"
commented/asked Romain Gary.

There was stony silence.

"That's the chance I have to take."

Gary went ahead, inquiring if he were taking precautions.

"Bobby said, with a shrug, 'There's no way of protecting a
country-stumping candidate. No way at all. You've just got to give
yourself to the people—and to trust them. From then on, it's just that
good old bitch, Luck.

"You have to have luck on your side to be elected President
of the United States. Either it's with you or it isn't.
I am pretty sure there will be an attempt on my life
sooner or later.

"Not so much for political reasons; I don't believe that.
Plain nuttiness, that's all. There's plenty of that around."

Next RFK plied Gary with a question: "Take de Gaulle—
how many attempts on his life has he survived, exactly?"

Gary: "Six or seven, I think."

RFK quietly laughed, "I told you. You can't make it without
that good old bitch, luck."[70]

RFK to Romain Gary, Another Version

Here's Arthur Schlesinger's text on what Gary said
upon meeting RFK in person:
"Somebody is going to try to kill you."

RFK replied that there are no guarantees against assassination.
"You've just got to give yourself to the people and to trust them,
and from then on . . . either (luck is) with you or it isn't.

I am pretty sure there'll be an attempt on my life sooner or later.
Not so much for political reasons. . . . Plain nuttiness, that's all."[71]

Yet Another Version

Robert: "There is no way to protect a candidate during the campaign.
    You must give yourself to the crowd,
    and from then on you must take your chances. . . . I know
    that there will be an attempt on my life sooner or later.
    Not so much for political reasons, but through contagion,
    through emulation."[72]

May 20
    There was a three-hour motorcade through
                    ebullient
                        Mexican-American neighborhoods
                                            in East LA.

    Then the motorcade reached Temple Isaiah.

    "Kennedy donned a yarmulke and spoke to the assembled
    Jewish voters . . . pledging support for Israel
    with remarks Sirhan may have later heard on all-news
                                station KFWB.[73]

The Clipping Found in Sirhan's Pocket

    When Kennedy pledged support for Israel
    at Temple Isaiah in LA, May 20

    wearing a yarmulke

    David Lawrence wrote a column about it,
    titled "Paradoxical Bob"

"Just the other day," the conservative Mr. Lawrence wrote,
"Sen. Robert F. Kennedy of New York made a speech in Los Angeles
which certainly was received with favor by Protestant, Catholic, and
Jewish groups which have been staunchly supporting the cause of
Israel against Egypt and the Arab Countries."

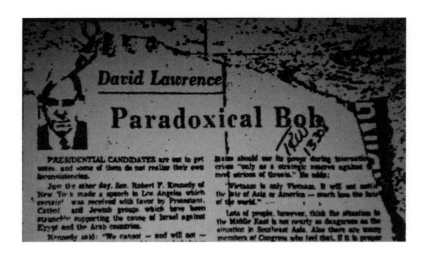

Sirhan, or someone, clipped Mr. Lawrence's column
"Paradoxical Bob," from the
May 26 *Pasadena Independent Star-News*,

and it was found in his shirt pocket when he was
arrested early June 5 at the Ambassador Hotel

Note however the notation on the clip, which
appears to me to be TRW
13308
(or 13306).

Why?

TRW is a well-known American defense contractor,
and with CIA connections,
so it's at least possible
that some of the assassination machinery
could have been activated there—

TRW's "Black Vault" Classified Communications Center

One Christopher Boyce, the son of a McDonnell Douglas
security officer, was hired in 1974 at So Cal aerospace company TRW
in Redondo Beach, California.

"We cannot—and will not—permit the Soviet Union to achieve an imbalance in the Middle East. We can and will fully assist Israel—with arms if necessary—to meet the threat of massive Soviet military build-ups. We cannot—and will not—render Israel defenseless in the face of aggression." May 16, 1968, Redondo Beach

Boyce was promoted to a "sensitive" job at the so-called
            "Black Vault"
        (a classified communications center).
They gave him a top secret clearance

Boyce says he began viewing cables from the CIA
discussing their eagerness to toss out the
    gov't of Australian Prime Minister Gough Whitlam

    apparently because of Whitlam's plan
    to close US military bases in Australia,
    including something called the Pine Gap
            secure communications facility.

    (Boyce went on to peddle US secrets to Russia.)

Again We Ask, Did the National Security Agency Have Robert Kennedy under Surveillance?

As we have previously indicated,
according to the *New York Times*
President Johnson received information about
Robert Kennedy's "personal activities and night life in Paris"
during a 1967 visit by RFK to Paris—
probably from the National Security Agency.

In an article dated 10-12-75, titled "Spying on U.S.
Travelers Reported for 2 Presidents" [Johnson and Nixon]
            by Nicholas Horrock,
The National Security Agency gave "private reports . . .
on what prominent Americans were doing and saying abroad,
apparently from electronic eavesdropping."

Did the NSA and other agencies
        keep on surveilling RFK
                after the trip to Paris,
including during his upcoming 1968 presidential campaign

and therefore knew well what he was telling friends—
that he was going to get to the bottom
                of his brother's killing?

NSA

RFK at a Synagogue in Portland
May 26

On May 26 Robert Kennedy spoke
              at a synagogue in Portland
              wearing a yarmulke
              & vowing unwavering commitment
                            to Israel.

        Kennedy's talk was seen around the nation,
        apparently also by Sirhan Sirhan
              who left the room
                    with his hands on his ears
                            and "almost weeping"

        (according to Jules Witcover in his book *85 Days*, page 218,
        who got the info from a report by an Egyptian writer named
        Mahmoud Abel-Hadi, who wrote he was told about
        Sirhan's leaving the room with hands on ears
                    from his brother, Shereif Sirhan).

On Monday, May 27
        RFK traveled with his campaign
              in two smaller planes
                    hopping across southern Oregon;

        the first stop was at Roseburg
        "the heart of hunting country,"
              as Jules Witcover described it.

RFK was calm-faced
as he spoke to about 1,500 gathered
on the steps of the Douglas County courthouse.

There were signs carried, such as
              "PROTECT YOUR RIGHTS TO KEEP AND BEAR ARMS"

Kennedy had a bill in the Senate.

The *New York Times* wrote that he said,
"I see signs about the guns. I'm wondering if any of you
              would like to come and explain."

A local handed Kennedy a petition against his bill,
which "forbids mail order sale of guns to the very young,
those with criminal records and the insane."

Kennedy commented: "All this legislation does
is keep guns from criminals and the demented and those too young.
With all the violence and murder and killings we've had in the
United States, I think you will agree that we must keep firearms
from people who have no business with guns or rifles."

Kennedy also said, "There's nothing in it that infringes
on any citizen's right to bear arms."

Widely watched CBS news anchor Walter Cronkite
reported on RFK's remarks in Roseburg, Oregon
on the lack of controls on guns bought through mail order
(such as Lee Harvey Oswald).

Investigating a Phone Call from 1963

In late May of '68
    RFK was flying up and down
        for votes in the California and Oregon primaries.

During a stop in Oregon
        Kennedy, according to Pete Noyes,
           in his book, *Legacy of Doubt*,
                told a friend that he intended to stop
off in Oxnard to try to learn anything more about
                the strange phone call.

George Sanders

    lived in Oregon,
    a radio newsman, or executive

Sanders had been a supporter of Nixon in
the 1960 presidential race. RFK kidded him
about this initially; they became friends.

George Sanders is the one RFK confided in about the
Oxnard phone call.[74]

Noyes, an executive at CBS television in LA, described
in his book *Legacy of Doubt* how

Kennedy during his campaign
expressed doubt
           about his brother's assassination.

RFK was bothered by an AP story from Oxnard, Calif.,
dated 11-23-63:

"A telephone company executive said that 20 minutes before President
Kennedy was assassinated a woman caller was overheard whispering:
      'The President is going to be killed.'
      Ray Sheehan, manager of the Oxnard division of General Telephone
Company, said the caller 'stumbled into our operator's circuits,'
perhaps by misdialing.
      Sheehan said the woman 'seemed to be a little bit disturbed.'
      Besides predicting the President's death, he said, she 'mumbled
several incoherent things.' Sheehan said the call was reported to the
Federal Bureau of Investigation in Los Angeles but not until after the
           President had been shot. Until then, he said, it appeared to
           have been just another crank call.

"Sheehan said there was no way to trace the call. All he could say
was that it originated in the Oxnard-Camarillo area some 50 miles
north of Los Angeles. The FBI in Los Angeles declined to comment.

"Sheehan said one telephone supervisor called another one onto her
line after getting the call. He said both supervisors heard the
woman say the President would be killed.

"Sheehan said the call was received at 10:10 a.m., Pacific time.
The President was shot in Dallas shortly after 10:30 a.m.
Sheehan said he doesn't think the caller was ever connected with
another party. He said she may not have known she had super-
visors on the line and may have just been talking to no one in
particular."[75]

RFK's Official Schedule for May 28, 1968 Shows as Follows:

that he was to arrive at the Santa Barbara airport
and drive to the Santa Barbara Courthouse
arriving at 3:30 p.m.
and then depart from the Santa Barbara Courthouse at 4:10
and drive to Ventura
to the Buenaventura Shopping Center.

Primary Day, Tuesday, May 28

Late Monday night RFK flew to Los Angeles and spent Tuesday,
the Oregon primary day,
touring the Santa Barbara-Ventura area.

After Kennedy and party flew into Oxnard on May 28,
Kennedy disappeared for two hours. When he returned, he said
he had lost his hat
and had spent the two hours looking for it.

He was delayed returning to Oregon
The official excuse was
foggy flying conditions.

As he toured Tuesday late in the afternoon,
he was told of the CBS sampling of voting in 400 key precincts:

he was losing.

He took the flight back to Oregon that evening;
aide Fred Dutton prepared for RFK a congratulatory telegram
to Senator McCarthy.

Kennedy Entering the Ballroom by Means of the Kitchen

He addressed his glum supporters at the ballroom
of the Benson Hotel in Portland.

The final vote: McC 44.7 %, RFK 38.8 %, Johnson 12.4, Humphrey 4.

He came down from his 7th floor suite, then entered the ballroom
by means of the hotel kitchen.[76]

Sirhan at Rosicrucian Lodge
May 28

The day of the Oregon primary
Sirhan attended for the first time
          a meeting at the Rosicrucian lodge in Pasadena.

"He volunteered for an experiment on touch sensations and was
blindfolded.
As the master, Ted Stevens touched his skin with different objects,
Sirhan had to guess how many there were. After the meeting, he browsed
the literature briefly,
          then left
                    as if he were in a hurry."

          Robo Robo.[77]

Huge Crowds in LA the Day after Oregon Primary
May 29

On John Kennedy's birthday, RFK and Ethel, staff
          & an entourage of reporters
                    flew to California, after the defeat in Oregon

     On the flight from Oregon
     Life magazine photographer Bill Eppridge
     took a picture of a smiling Ethel
               carrying a large birthday cake with lit candles
               for bodyguard Bill Barry

     down the aisle past balloons and crepe paper bunting
     attached to the plane walls
                    to bring a morale-boosting good time to
                                        the sad flight.

     That day, RFK traveled in a motorcade
     through downtown LA, through Watts, East LA,

Morale booster—Ethel carrying Bill Barry's birthday cake in the plane back to LA the morning after the loss in Oregon

attracting huge huge throngs,
100s walking beside the candidate's vehicle
(which was trailed by a convertible full of photographers).

RFK ran back to the photographers
                    in the convertible
and shouted "Los Angeles is my Resurrection City!"

            then trotted back to his waving & greeting.[78]

Just a Few Days Available for the Killers

When Kennedy drove through the tens of thousands
in LA on May 29,
        he'd campaigned by then
                for all or part of just ten days in California.

May 30–31, 1968

Memorial Day RFK
        covered cities in the Central Valley.

He and Ethel were in
San Francisco on Friday, May 31,

staying at the Fairmont Hotel on Nob Hill,
where he spent hours
cramming for the upcoming debate
                        with Gene McCarthy.

Kennedy-McCarthy Debate
June 1

    Then Saturday evening, the debate,
    a panel of 3 journalists asking Qs,

    6:30 California time
                but 9:30 in the eager East.

Resurrection City

RFK did fairly well,
                the histories say.

In the evening after the debate,
there was a star- & celebrity-packed
                "gala"
                in San Francisco.

Bob and Ethel paid a visit but left early,
                likely driven by Rosey Grier
                                in a station wagon.

Sirhan Wanting to Purchase Ammo

During the day of the Kennedy-McCarthy debate,
Sirhan Sirhan plus two "friends" came into the
        Lock Stock and Barrel gun shop in
        San Gabriel
                wanting to purchase some armor-piercing
                .357 magnum ammo

(maybe for a hit through limo glass?).

        They didn't have any, and so
        Sirhan purchased four boxes of .22 caliber bullets
                for $3.99.

Sirhan at Corona Police Shooting Range,
Saturday, June 1

That same day, June 1, Sirhan later "recalled
being taken to the [Corona Police Firing Range],
where the range master
        showed him how to shoot
        at human targets & vital organs."

He signed the register
accompanied by a man
        with turned-down mustache
                & foreign accent

who refused to sign in
                or identify himself.[79]

The man accompanying Sirhan to the Police Firing Range
fit the description "of the strange man with the
                turned-down mustache and foreign accent"

who had begun working on his mind
in a prison-like hospital
        where he spent two weeks
            after his fall from a horse in September of 1966.[80]

(FBI reports on the assassination
verify that Sirhan Sirhan did shoot
        at the Corona Police Firing Range on June 1.)

Shortwave Radio in the Nights before the Shooting

"Mr. Sirhan was an avid enthusiast of short wave radios.
He had a short wave radio in his bedroom,

        "and spent most nights before the assassination
        communicating on his short wave radio to third parties.

"Mr. Sirhan frequently entered a hypnotic state
while communicating with other parties
            on the short wave radio.
            While in trance Mr. Sirhan would automatically
write down what was communicated to him,
and subsequently was amnesic for the content
            of his automatic writing in the spiral notebooks."[81]

The History of Sirhan's .22

Mrs. Dana Tulita Westlake
        to the FBI on 6/17/68:

Her father, Mr. Hertz, originally purchased
the .22 cal 8-shot Iver-Johnson
        in 1965
during the Watts Riots.

Her mother
around January '67
gave it to her.

Revolver still in a box &
wrapped in black oily paper.

She hid it from children
in her attic.

In Sept. or Oct. of '67
her husband remodeled their
house & they removed the roof—

so she purged the attic
& "since her neighbor's son,
George Charles Erhard, Jr.,
collected guns, she gave him the revolver."

It had never been fired.[82]

Then according to an FBI interview dated 6-7-68,
George Erhard, Jr.
        related that he had possessed the .22 till
        around February 15, 1968,

        "when he sold it to a fellow employee at
        the F. C. Nash Company, a department store . . .
        Pasadena, known to him as 'Joe'"
Erhard identified a photo of Munir Bishara Sirhan
                as the "Joe"
                        to whom he sold the pistol
                                for $25.
(Munir had previously asked Erhard
        if he had a gun for sale.)[83]

In another FBI interview, also dated 6-7-68,
William Price stated that early February '68
he'd been visiting George Erhard

and went with Erhard to sell a .22
to someone named "Joe"
        on Howard St. in Pasadena.

Iver-Johnson gun

Erhard showed the weapons to "Joe"
& the FBI report states: "Price recalls that 'Joe'
stated that he wanted his brother to see the pistol
& his brother looked over the pistol. . . .

He identified a photograph of Sirhan Sirhan
as being identical with 'Joe's' brother."[84]

Sunday Morning, June 2

Sunday morning RFK taped a television interview in SF
during which he wished that after the primary
he & McCarthy would "somehow join
& try to bring together"
all the antiwar movements.

After the interview
Bob and Ethel returned to the Fairmont
then attended mass in St. Mary's Church
a few blocks down steep Nob Hill
from the hotel.

Ethel wanted to walk
up the steep sidewalk back to the hotel
after the mass.[85]

CIA robo-courier Candy Jones recalls
being at the Fairmont Hotel
in early June 1968
& seeing Rosey Grier, famed football star
& bodyguard to Robert & Ethel

in the lounge of the Fairmont.

Jones recounted that Grier was
driving Ethel in a station wagon
to the television station,
apparently for the interview.

Jones also asserted that she saw a doctor
with a Viennese accent—

Ethel

"He sounded like Otto Preminger"—
          being driven by Grier in a station wagon.

This was the same doctor, she said, who had hypnotized Sirhan
          according to what she had been told by her
                    programmer,
                    Dr. Albert Carsen.[86]

A Genuine Robo-Washer with a Viennese Accent

One prominent gov't hypnosis expert with a Viennese accent[87]
was Martin Orne, active in the CIA's
MKULTRA research program.[88]
Orne later was the "Principal Investigator" from 1968–1971
for an 86-page report on hypnosis and other robo-topics
          for the Office of Naval Research.[89]

          It brings to thought
          the possibility
          that Candy Jones was involved

          or maybe even was programmed to shoot
                    RFK,
                    maybe on the way to or from
                    the television station

                    or on the short drive by Rosey Grier
                    down the steep hillside
                              from the hotel to the church for mass

          after the television interview.

                    Crazy idea?
                    Nothing too crazy
                              for 1968.

After Mass the Kennedys Flew to Orange County

Then they flew to Southern California
for a Strawberry Festival in Orange County,

The Magic Kingdom

after which they took 6 of their kids
                    to Disneyland
where they were surrounded by unexpecting
excited tourists as they took a ride on
                    "Pirates of the Caribbean."⁹⁰

They wound up later that day at
their suite of rooms on the 5th floor at
RFK's headquarters at
the elegant Ambassador Hotel
with its long horseshoe-shaped
                    front driveway.

Juan Romero

A 17-year-old named Juan Romero
worked in the room service staff at the hotel,
traveling to work after classes at Roosevelt High.

Young Romero was strongly attracted to RFK.
He recalled JFK's photos on the walls of houses
                    back in Mexico
next to Pope John Paul & the crucifix
& he very much appreciated that the candidate
had marched with
        California farm workers,

so he paid a colleague on the room service staff
for the right to bring RFK's food orders to his room.

On one of the nights—it was probably Sunday
                    after the trip to Disneyland—

Juan Romero pushed the food cart into Kennedy's room
and found himself next to the Candidate.

"He shook my hand as hard as anyone had ever shaken it,"
Romero later recalled. "I walked out of there
                    20 feet tall,
        thinking, 'I'm not just a busboy, I'm a human being.'
        He made me feel that way."

Sirhan on June 2

He drove his mother to church,
then in the afternoon tried to
fire at the Corona Police Range
> but couldn't because only large-bore weapons
> were fired on Sundays.

He apparently purchased a *Los Angeles Times*,
noticed a rally for RFK at the Ambassador.

He stopped off at a place called Stan's Drive-In
for cherry pie & coffee,

but at the Ambassador it was so crowded
Sirhan couldn't get in.

He waited with the overflow crowd
> by a fountain.

(Apparently Sirhan actually saw RFK at the rally.
At his trial, he testified how, when
he saw Robert Kennedy,
> "my whole attitude toward him changed
> because every time before, I associated him
> with the Phantom jet bombers that he was
> going to send to Israel and I pictured him
> > as a villain . . .
> but when I saw him that night
> he looked like a saint to me."

He denied in court going to the Ambassador
looking for a place to shoot.)[91]

TRW Clipping for June 2 in Sirhan's Pocket the Night of the Shooting

Also in Sirhan's possession at the time of the shooting was a newspaper
ad for a Kennedy rally, 5 inches by 5 inches,

> You and your friends are cordially invited
> To come to see and hear

SENATOR ROBERT KENNEDY
On Sunday, June 2, 1968
At 8:00 p.m.
Cocoanut Grove
Ambassador Hotel, Los Angeles
Leon M. Cooper, Treasurer
Jesse Unruh, Chairman

This clipping also had TRW handwritten upon it
(and with a number following the letters "TRW").

The Kitchen Route

An attorney from DC named Roger Lewis was working
as a volunteer advance man for the campaign. Lewis told
the FBI, "he had been with the Kennedy party at Disneyland
(on Sunday, June 2), and at two rallies held in and outside the
Cocoanut Grove in Los Angeles, California. Lewis said the kitchen
route in the Ambassador Hotel had been suggested and shown
to the late Senator Robert Kennedy as a good way to get from the
Cocoanut Grove to the Palm Court prior to one of the above rallies.
Lewis was with the late Senator Robert Kennedy and Ethel Kennedy
when this was done."[92]

Head RFK Advance Man Jerry Bruno
Also Described How the Use of the
Ambassador Kitchen as a Route Evolved:

"I remember that we had had a reception on the Sunday before the
primary (June 2), and Bob's cousin Polly Fitzgerald had asked us to take
him through the kitchen because the crowds would have been
impossible.
I said to him then: 'Senator, do me a favor and go through the kitchen

because Polly asked and I promised her I'd do it.' Kennedy just grinned
and said, 'I'll do it.'

Polly Fitzgerald
was a cousin by marriage to JFK and RFK
& she had a legendary status as a campaigner.

When JFK defeated Henry Cabot Lodge
for US Senate in 1952,
    Lodge blamed "those damn
    tea parties" hosted by Polly Fitzgerald, some 33 parties
    in all. Polly also campaigned for JFK in 1960,

    and for RFK in 1968
    she organized the groups of young women
                    on the Hostess Committee
    and was staying in the Ambassador.

    Jerry Bruno continued: "So that Tuesday night (when RFK was shot)
        the kitchen route was familiar to everyone.

    "After he got through his speech, he saw a hand in the crowd
    guiding him—
    he always looked for a familiar face and would follow—and one of the
    hotel officials was there waving to him, and they went through the
    kitchen, where Sirhan was waiting."[93]

Writer Walter Sheridan Walks with Bob and Ethel through the Ambassador Kitchen on June 2

    Campaign operative Walter Sheridan arranged for farm-worker leader
    César Chávez to speak personally with RFK
                    the night of the election.
    Two days before that, Sunday, June 2, Sheridan told the FBI later,
        "a reception was held for
Senator Kennedy and his wife at the Cocoanut Grove at the
    Ambassador Hotel. On this occasion the hotel was very
    crowded and Sheridan accompanied Senator Kennedy from
    his room to the receptions and they were taken through the
    serving kitchen to avoid the crowds. Sheridan was of the
    opinion that Sirhan may have observed this and been able
    to have positioned himself to be near Kennedy
                    after Kennedy spoke following the election."[94]

Many Stars and Entertainers Perform at the Ambassador's Cocoanut Grove on June 2

The FBI interviewed Joseph Scanlon, of Rhode Island,
who, with his wife attended the Cocoanut Grove June 2 festivities:

"He said that the only item of interest that he could recall
was that on the evening of June 2, 1968, a Sunday evening,
a reception was held for Senator Kennedy in the Cocoanut
Grove Club. He said that many stars of the stage and screen
and other celebrities were present and were entertaining. He
said that he . . . noted that a big stocky man about 6 feet 2 inches,
250 pounds, dark hair, large features kept trying to get behind
the stage area. He was told several times to leave the area but
would not, until finally he, Scanlon,
and the other men told him to get out of there and pointed him out
to other aides; and he was removed from the area. He said that he
did not know of his identity and that this was the only incident he saw
prior to the assassination at any time that caused suspicion on his
part.[95]

Mary Sirhan Argues over Turning Over Money to Sirhan from Horse-Fall Settlement
June 3

Sirhan had handed over $1,000 in hundred-dollar bills
(out of the $1,705 Argonaut settlement)
to his mother to keep for him.

At different times, he asked for some back
till Mary Sirhan held only four $100 bills

Around June 3, Sirhan asked her for $300,
and the mother later told LAPD
that he said he was going to use the money
to get some sort of job.

Mary Sirhan threw the remaining $400 at her son
and shouted, "Take it all and blow it on the horses!"

Sirhan picked up the scattered C-notes, kept $300 & gave $100
to his mother, saying,
"This is for you mother."[96]

LAPD interview 7-2-68, Addendum for Progress
Report of August 2, 1968, in Philip Melanson
RFK archive, UMass Dartmouth

The request for $300 from Sirhan's mom
is the same amount
        as a guy named Jerry Owen says he wanted
        for selling a horse to Sirhan
                around the same day.

FBI Files on Oliver B. Owen aka Jerry Owen Who Said He'd Picked Up Sirhan Sirhan on June 3, 1968 Hitchhiking in LA

Owen claimed to have picked up Sirhan and one other
when he was in LA on June 3 to pick up some sporting goods.

He was "driving a 1942 Chevrolet pick-up truck which had a
large palomino horse on the hood." Two young men
approached him at a stop light on Hill Street, and one asked
if he was going out Wilshire Boulevard, and Owen said he was,
and one asked if they could ride in the back. Okay.

They went west on Wilshire; at the intersection of Vermont and
Wilshire, Owen stopped for traffic light, and both got out.
Number One went to a bus stop nearby and greeted a man and
a woman. Number Two started to follow Number One but came back
to Owen's truck. He opened the door and asked "to ride up
front to continue toward Hollywood." Owen nodded okay, so
in came Number Two. They left Number One at the bus stop.

"During the ride, the conversation of horses came up, and Number
Two asked Owen if he owned horses and he said that he did.
        Number Two remarked that he used to work at
        a race track and at present needed a horse.

        "Owen said that he had horses for sale and offered to
        sell him one for $300. They talked some more about
        buying and selling a horse and Number Two asked Owen
        if he could stop for a short time so that he could see
        a friend who worked in a kitchen nearby where they were
        at the moment.

"Owen said he turned off Wilshire Boulevard onto a side street, the name of which he does not know. He described the street as a dead end street that was several blocks long. He parked the truck and waited while Number Two went to see his friend.

"After a wait of about ten minutes, Owen decided that Number Two was not going to return so he began to turn the truck around and leave. As he was doing this, he observed Number Two come through an opened gate in a fence behind which was a tall building with many rooms. Owen said that he was later advised by a police officer of the Los Angeles Police Department, that this building was the Ambassador Hotel.

"When Number Two got back in the truck, Owen again began making conversation and asked the man if he was Mexican. He told him that he was not, saying that he was from Jordan having either come from Jordan thirteen years ago or when he was thirteen years old.

"Owen could not recall which he said. He said his name was Joe and gave a surname which Owen did not understand, but which sounded like Zaharias. Owen said at about this time, he was arriving at his destination, that is a shoe shop and tailor shop where he was going to leave the boxing shoes and the robe for O'Riley to have shamrocks put on.

"He said that he parked the truck in the Hollywood Ranch Market's lot and took the shoes to a bootblack named Smitty. While he was conducting this business, Number Two stayed in the truck. He returned to the truck, and drove a few blocks and let Number Two out on the corner of Wilshire near a bowling alley and a go-go topless bar. Before he left Number Two agreed to meet Owen at 11:00 p.m. on the same corner at which time he would have the money to buy the horse.

"He met the fighter O'Riley that evening and left him shortly before 11:00 p.m. and arrived back at the agreed meeting place and observed a 1958 or 1959 Chevrolet, off-white in color, in which there were three men and a girl. Owen believed that one of the men and the girl may have been the same couple that Number One was talking to earlier at the bus stop.

"He could not get a good look at the second man in the car. Number Two came over to the truck and showed him a $100 bill saying he would have the rest of the money the next day early in the morning. Owen told him he would stay overnight in Los Angeles and pointed out a hotel which was either St. Mark's or St. Martin, which would be where he would stay.

"He registered at this hotel as J. C. Owen and requested the clerk give him a call at 8:00 a.m. However, he said he was up at 7:00 a.m. and just as he was leaving the hotel he received a call from a man asking if he was the man with the pick-up and horse. Owen acknowledged that he was and said he would meet him in a few minutes at the truck. As he was going to the truck he saw the same white car as before parked at the curb and Number One and the girl whom he saw before, were sitting in the car. The man who had been at the bus stop was standing by the truck and as Owen approached he said 'Joe could not make it.'

"He offered Owen a $100 bill and asked if he could bring the horse to the same location that night at which time the remainder of the money would be available. Owen did not take the money and explained that he would not be able to deliver the horse that night because of a prior commitment that he had in Oxnard. He left the man, giving him his business card, which had his home address and an unlisted telephone number and requested that Joe call him if he was interested in the horse.

"Owen then proceeded to Oxnard on business and returned to Los Angeles the morning of June 5, 1967 [meaning 1968].

"Owen said he went to the Coliseum Hotel to see a man, Bert, who owns the restaurant and bar in the hotel. He had, at this time, three ponies in his trailer, which he had obtained in Oxnard. While in the restaurant he learned

of the Kennedy shooting hearing it on television.
Someone gave him a copy of the 'Hollywood Citizen News,'
which contained a picture of Sirhan B. Sirhan, which he
noted looked like the man he knew as Joe. He discussed this
with Bert and other of his friends in the restaurant
and they suggested that he go to the Los Angeles
Police Department, University Station, which was nearby,
and tell them what had occurred. At first he said that he
did not want to do this, but they convinced him that as
a good citizen this would be the thing to do. That same day,
he went to the Police Department and gave them the same
story that he was now relating. He said that he was at the
station from about 2:00 p.m. to 7:00 p.m."

A couple of phone calls were received at his residence
on June 6, answered by his wife and daughter.
On each occasion, the caller hung up without speaking.
"When the phone rang again, Owen said he answered it
and the caller said 'Keep your mother blankety blank mouth
shut about the horse deal.'" The caller was an unfamiliar man.
On June 22, Owen said he'd received another call, with the
caller saying "Keep your mother blankety blank mouth shut
or your family may be hurt." That was the last threatening call
Owen's number received.

A factual account or false muffins of the meadow?[97]

pages 295–301 FBI interview with Owen 7-8-68 in FBI files
in yellow three-ring binder #Gamma
in RFK FBI bankers boxes in gray baby barn

This is covered extensively, with oodles of additional details,
in Jonn Christian's and William Turner's
book *The Assassination of Robert F. Kennedy.*

The Final Day of Campaigning
June 3, a Monday

It saw a long and extremely tiring series of plane rides, motorcades
& rallies up and down the state of California.

First RFK and Ethel flew from LA to San Francisco
for a motorcade.

In the convertible

Landing in SF
the RFK caravan sped downtown,
then late morning to Chinatown,
where it slowed down
for handshakes and brief remarks.

The streets were three-deep in onlookers
as Ethel and Robert stood
on the backseat, waving.

About three blocks into Chinatown
there were about six
sharp explosions—
big firecrackers, like cherry bombs.

Ethel sat down quickly, hunched over,
but RFK stayed standing.

The motorcade went onward to Fisherman's Wharf
where RFK spoke at DiMaggio's Restaurant.

Then they flew to Long Beach,
where 6,000 supporters filled a park.

Then they drove through Watts,
then through Venice,
where RFK asked for a ginger ale.[98]

The Mamas and Papas Perform
on a Flatbed Truck
June 3

Peter Lawford had asked John Phillips
to write a Mamas & Papas tune
to the RFK campaign.
He didn't write one,
but on June 3 the Mamas and Papas
rode through LA
on the back of a flatbed truck,

"Singing songs," as Phillips writes in his autobiography,
"for his rally that day."

Fireworks in Chinatown

Police Ticketing Kennedy's Motorcade

In Los Angeles the police weren't all that friendly,
as traced in a later FBI report:

Peter P. Smith was the head advance man
    for RFK in Los Angeles. He ran the motorcades

    He told the FBI that RFK did not have
    police escorts and adequate protection in LA
    as laid out in an FBI report in their RFK "Kensalt" investigation:

    "He said that when Senator Kennedy and
    his party
        came off the freeway into
        LA they were met by the police
    and told that they could not
                run any lights.

    He said that after they proceeded
           several blocks,
    the crowds began to gather each
        time the motorcade
           stopped for a light

    and that finally the police
        returned and because they
    were halting traffic, they, the police,
        took them straight on through
    the traffic lights to their destination
        in downtown Los Angeles.

    He said that then the
           police issued the
    motorcade citations for
        passing the traffic lights."[99]

Final Rally of the Campaign

After a 12-hour day
the final event of the campaign
a late-night rally at the El Cortez Hotel in San Diego,

where friends the singers Rosemary Clooney
& Andy Williams entertained the crowd.

The crowd so huge it had to be divided in two,
so that RFK delivered two separate speeches.

    After the first one, he walked off stage
    and sat in a chair,
    face buried into his hands.

    Bill Barry and Rafer Johnson escorted him to a men's room.
    He pulled himself together

for the second exhausted speech,
        then the campaign came to a close,

        after which the entourage flew to Los Angeles.

    During the flight
        Robert invited Rosemary Clooney to
        sit with Ethel and him.

Pattern of Using Freight Elevators

    The pattern of using back elevators
        and freight elevators continued:

    "The candidate and party left the (El Cortez Hotel)
        in a wide freight elevator
        that got stuck a few times before
        discharging its weary passengers."[100]

Deciding to Stay in Malibu

Though Kennedy headquarters for the California primary
was at the Ambassador Hotel in Los Angeles
(located at 3400 Wilshire Boulevard downtown),

where Ethel and Robert had a suite of rooms
and key staff members also had rooms, nevertheless,

after the exhaustion of San Diego, the Kennedys first
returned to the Ambassador Hotel
then, according to future Senator John Glenn
(active in the California primary for RFK),
decided to stay with John and Evans Frankenheimer
     on Malibu Colony Road in Malibu.[101]

  The Kennedys were driven to
     101 Malibu Colony Road.
  Six out of ten of the kids were on hand

Frankenheimer, the noted director of such films as
The Manchurian Candidate, Seven Days in May,
Grand Prix and *Birdman of Alcatraz,*
had been hired to shoot footage of RFK and his campaign
    beginning in April for the Indiana campaign
    & continuing through early June.

(It's possible that his robo-controls
  sent Sirhan after Kennedy
  that grueling June 3 day.

One book reports Sirhan told an investigator
for his defense team that he had
350 miles on his DeSoto that day. Enough to get to
San Diego and back. San Diego, where an
exhausted Kennedy spoke to the overflow crowd
    at the El Cortez Hotel.[102])

Robert Kennedy's Final Day
June 4, 1968

John Lennon rerecorded the lead vocal
for "Revolution"
  lying flat on his back
    at the studio on Abbey Road.

That same day Soviet tanks and troops
    shoved inward into Czechoslovakia,

Exhaustion

                              ostensibly for maneuvers
but excuses were found for leaving them.

Sirhan awakened around 8.
He had planned to go to the horse races
                              at Hollywood Park
and also planned that evening to attend a meeting
in Pasadena of the Rosicrucian sect.

His brother Munir
        saw him as he was going to work
        purchasing a newspaper from a street corner vender
                        in Pasadena.

LA DA's time track on Sirhan for June 3–4, 1968 says:
"During the two weeks prior to the assassination,
Sirhan had been going to the horse races and betting almost daily . . .
(and) he planned to attend the races on election day at Hollywood
Park."[103]

But he purchased a newspaper
& had no taste for the horses running that day,
                        so opted to go target shooting

(was he urged to do this by his programmer(s)?).

He drove to the East Pasadena Firearms Co.
& purchased six or seven boxes of Federal long rifle .22s.

Then Sirhan had coffee at a Denny's
& on to the San Gabriel Valley Gun Range
                on Fish Canyon Rd
                        in Duarte, outside LA.

(Possible time discrepancy—Sirhan should have arrived, say,
around 10–10:30 a.m. Was he intercepted by his programmer(s)
and ordered to the practice range?)

        (The site of the San Gabriel Valley Gun Club
        [closed in 2007] is now a parking area
        for the Fish Creek trailhead
                leading to Fish Creek Falls.)

The shooting range was north of Pasadena,
             an easy drive for Sirhan in his '56 DeSoto
             who arrived about 11:30,

paid a $2-dollar admission price
& set up his target and stayed there
             until five p.m. when the range master announced
             the range was closing.

During the afternoon Sirhan used up all his Federal .22 bullets
& purchased a few more boxes from the range master

Sirhan was asked by another young man (a college student)
why he was firing high-velocity Mini-Mags
                 just for target shooting

Sirhan answered, "They're supposed to be the best brand."

The college student replied, "They're for hunting. They're way
too strong for this gun. . . ."

When the student departed at 3, Sirhan
stopped firing the Mini-Mags.

Later Sirhan spoke with Claudia Williams, on hand to
fire a new .22 cal revolver she'd gotten for Christmas.

She and her husband had arrived around 3:50, and husband
went to the rifle range to fire.

She had difficulty pulling the trigger and asked Sirhan
        for help. Sirhan showed her how to fire
        & shot about 18 rounds of his high-powered Mini-Mags
            from Claudia's revolver. Then she
            fired about 16 from Sirhan's.

      They chatted around 20 minutes
      Her husband then returned
          and then circa 5,
          (according to her interview with the FBI)
          the range master
          announced closing
               and the couple departed.

Another Version of Claudia Williams interaction with Sirhan Sirhan at the Gun Range

The woman named
Claudia Williams and her husband
came target shooting

They claimed to have arrived
around 4 p.m.

The husband shot a rifle.
Claudia, attractive and worked at a topless bar,
asked Sirhan to help her fire her pistol.

He complied.

According to the shooting range's "range master,"
Everett Buckner (who told the same story on two
occasions to the FBI, June 8 & 12, '68),

Buckner said that not long after Sirhan
had signed into the range

a couple entered, it was circa 10:00 to 10:30 a.m.

The man began firing the rifle on the rifle range
& the woman, young, blonde & good-looking,
was having trouble firing her .22.

Buckner stated to the FBI that when Sirhan
offered to help the woman,
she exclaimed, "God damn you, you son of a bitch,
get out of here or they'll recognize us."

Buckner stated that Sirhan did not depart,
                                    but continued to assist her.

(LAPD later claimed Buckner failed a polygraph test.
After the test, Buckner stated
        "I think it's true. I think she said it.
                    I still think she said it."[104])

When Sirhan left the range, one account said he had loaded his .22
with bullets called Mini-Mags.[105]

(Witnesses to the later shooting
said it appeared Sirhan was firing off blanks.)

Sirhan Told Researcher He Tried Firing Blanks at the Firing Range June 4

Lynn Mangan, indefatigable Sirhan researcher,
has written about "Sirhan's telling me that he met a
young man at the Fish Canyon Firing Range and that the
young man had received a gun for his eighteenth birthday.
He was firing blanks and shared those blanks with Sirhan.
That is not to say that Sirhan had blanks in his gun when
he left the firing range."

And this: "Sirhan told me that he fired blanks in his gun
at the gun range on June fourth."[106]

—Lynn Mangan, "Plain Talk 3: September 11, 2011,"
at sirhansresearcher.com

FBI States Sirhan at Shooting Range Till 3 p.m.

The FBI alleges Sirhan was at Shooting Range 11 a.m.–ca 3 p.m

Sirhan "at San Gabriel Valley Gun Club from approximately
11:00 a.m. to 3:00 p.m. Bob's Restaurant, Colorado (Blvd) and
Pasadena City College Cafeteria about 6:00 p.m.–7:15 p.m."

Question: if he departed at 3, what did he do between
3 p.m. and 6 p.m.?

The Malibu Surf

The ocean at Malibu
churned in the fog
the morning of the win

187

where Robert and Ethel lay sleeping
in a house overlooking the
ceaseless peace of the beach.

A brief night striving to restore his vim
in the tiredness of nearly nonstop
      plane rides, motorcades, rallies, speeches,
      chatting with the press, phone calls,
      staff meetings, & other body-bashing stresses

in an "On the Eve" set of hours
before the sea-like pressure of Time
bore him forward to
further contests for delegates,
such as the New York primary two weeks ahead
& a convention in Chicago.

The struggle for delegates
was still a triangulation of

      Kennedy

      McCarthy Humphrey

McCarthy was not about to drop out,
especially with his strength among New York's antiwar activists.

It was a strange equation: the big-city bosses
and state chairs
      clutched many a delegate to their chests.

Mayor Richard Daley of Chicago, for instance
had a batch of clout

& RFK, after California
was going to have to convince Mr. Daley, & others
that Humphrey was not the anointed.

Goofing in the Tiredness

The Frankenheimers had given
Ethel and Robert their own bedroom
where they could rest for a few hours.

Family

RFK at 42
had the wiriness of a coiled spring
& the stamina of a star athlete in service of the Polis.
They said he slept only four hours a night
but the weeks nonstop had sapped him.

You know how it is
You boing awake,
mind pulsing with stuff to do,
calls to make, issues to jot & plans to polish,

plus eating at the craw of his psyche
the death of his brother
and vengeance on those who had done it.

Ethel was pregnant with their 11th child
      (Rory, born the coming December).
She too had bundles of energy,
which she brought to the campaign
                  with friend-rousing grace.

Oceanus lay churning just feet from his window,
gray, grim, glimmering and glorious!

It was cold to swim at Malibu
in the skin-chilling surf and a ten-mile wind
at John and Evans' portion of beach.

First RFK, Ethel and
six of their ten children had lunch.

      Joining them was Theodore White
      in the midst of his research for a book
                  on the '68 race.

Then RFK in trunks
went with 12-yr-old David and 3-yr-old Max
            to the water's edge
            where he helped build a sand castle.

He spotted David
being pulled down by an undertow
            and dashed into the churn to save him,

father and son
both a bit bruised from the saving.

After swimming in the ocean,
there was more fun in the Frankenheimers' pool.

RFK's flashy pink & green Hawaiian trunks
were in the bedroom lavatory sink

where they remained
till after the shooting when some aides
early in the a.m.
arrived to retrieve his personal items.

A Brief Political Chat

Edward Kennedy, Richard Goodwin and Fred Dutton arrived
& there was a bit of political talk,

then the candidate took a nap.

Richard Goodwin was getting some food from a buffet
when he noticed RFK spread out across two chairs by the pool

getting a restless shut-eye.

Just after 3 P.M.

For that afternoon John Frankenheimer
had arrayed a row of television sets in the house
to watch how the election was evolving

At Malibu they learned the first exit polls.
CBS had taken "spot checks" of 200 sample precincts
around noon
and close to 3 p.m. phoned the
results to press secretary Frank Mankiewicz:

49% for Kennedy
less for McCarthy

A couple of close RFK aides
bought themselves bright-hued hippie attire
        to wear to the victory party
            that night at a discotheque called The Factory
            owned by Pierre Salinger & other
                  well-known Democrats
                  (such as Sammy Davis, Jr.).

Speechwriter Richard Goodwin Recalls June 4

"After breakfast, Bobby called to say he was spending the day
at John Frankenheimer's Malibu Beach home.
                Would I come and join him?"

"The living room of the Frankenheimer house and the adjoining
dining room were divided by a glass wall from a swimming pool
and a broad patio. Beyond was the gentle-surfed beach.
Ethel Kennedy was seated, talking with Teddy White and Mrs.
      Frankenheimer, but the candidate was not there.
      Going into the next room for the buffet lunch,
           I turned casually toward the pool.

"Robert Kennedy was stretched out across two chairs
in the sunlight, he head hanging limply over the chair frame;
his unshaven face was deeply lined, and his lips slightly parted.

"There was no movement. I felt a sudden spasm of fear.
        But it swiftly receded. He was sleeping, only sleeping. . . .

"By the time the telephone brought the first
        tentative vote projections, Kennedy and Fred Dutton
        had joined the group in the Frankenheimer living room.
One of the networks, having surveyed voters in key precincts
        as they left the polling places,
           was now predicting a 49-41 victory over McCarthy. . . .

"'They were pretty accurate in the other primaries,' Kennedy
remarked.

"'But not in Oregon,' said Dutton.

"'We lost all the undecided there,' Kennedy replied, then added,
'Maybe they won't break away from us here.
　　　　　　　If only we can push up our percentage a point or two.'

"It seemed then that the extra point or two would
make all the difference. We all believed that it was not enough
for Kennedy to win in California.
　　　　　　　In order to soften the blow of his Oregon defeat,
　　　　　　　we felt he had to win big, and that meant more
than 50 percent of the vote, with 40 percent or less going to
McCarthy. . . .

"We talked idly, reminisced, discussed future strategy,
as if the big victory were already in—not because we were sure,
　　　　　　　but because that's the only way politicians can talk.

　　　"But Kennedy was so tired that even the easily familiar
　　　shoptalk came haltingly, and he soon went back
　　　　　　　to the bedroom for a nap
　　　　　　　while I drove to my hotel to draft the
　　　　　　　victory statement."[107]

The Dinner at the Frankenheimers'

One account has John & Evans Frankenheimer planning an early
dinner and inviting some guests over.

According to Robert Blair Kaiser's book *RFK Must Die*,
the guest list included director Roman Polanski,
whose movie *Rosemary's Baby*
　　　　　　　was selling a lot of tickets,
and his wife Sharon Tate.

Other guests were future head of Disney Pictures Frank Wells
and his wife Luanne, plus actress Anjanette Comer, nightclub owner
Brian Morris, set designer Richard Sylbert, and a woman named
Sarah Hudson, who was living with Sylbert at the time.

　　　(I emailed Mr. Kaiser a few years ago, questioning him
　　　as to his source for the 6-4 dinner in Malibu, and he replied

that Frankenheimer himself told him about the
guest list and the early meal at his Malibu house.
Mr. Kaiser's email, dated 5-31-2002, reads: "Ed, yes,
John Frankenheimer was my source on the dinner
and the dinner guests. As Frankenheimer recalled the
story, it seems hardly likely that he could have
gotten the dates confused. He said he and Bobby
attended the dinnner, then hit Pacific Coast Highway
and into LA on the I-10, to arrive at the Ambassador.
I don't put the time down for that arrival, but I am now
thinking, since you ask, that it couldn't have been any
earlier than 9 p.m. and possibly even later, because there
was still some uncertainty about the election outcome
when they arrived. So they could well have had dinner
from 7 to 8 p.m. or even 9.")[108]

Perhaps Tate, Polanski and the others
were invited for dinner,

but RFK had been too eager to get to the hotel,
so Frankenheimer quickly took him

before, or just as, the guests arrived?

Or, maybe they arrived, but Robert Kennedy
had already departed for the Ambassador?

Robert Kennedy: His Life by Evan Thomas
does not mention an early dinner in Malibu.

Nor does *RFK: A Candid Biography of Robert F. Kennedy,* by
C. David Heymann.

(I wrote Roman Polanski in Paris seeking clarification
but no reply.)

Evans Frankenheimer Denies Dinner Occurred

Evans Frankenheimer, widow of John Frankenheimer,
informed me by email during the writing of this book,
that there was no dinner served to Sharon Tate, Roman Polanski,
Richard Sylbert, Sarah Hudson and the others. She writes:

"There was no dinner scheduled at our house in Malibu
on the evening of the Democratic Primary, June 4th, 1968.
The Kennedys wanted privacy during their stay at our house.
There was, however, a large party scheduled at The Factory
after the primary. The people you mentioned in your letter
were on that guest list. It was not our private party and

Sharon and Roman had been invited as guests of Dick Sylbert—
the set designer."

In addition, Richard Sylbert's widow, Sharmagne St. John,
checked Sylbert's day books, and reported the following entry by Sylbert:
"On the afternoon of June 5th (actually the 4th), 1968 we all got into
our respective Limousines outside the Frankenheimer's house
and drove cautiously downtown to the Ambassador Hotel
and walked into the Presidential Suites. One group disappeared with
Bobby, while myself and Sarah [Hudson], along with several others
went into a nearby suite. There were several old friends
already ensconced there, Budd Schulberg, and as I remember,
George Plimpton along with the mob of the faithful,
chatting and watching the returns on the TV sets in each room."

So, what is the answer? The past is like quicksand.

RFK Restless in the Late Afternoon of June 4

RFK took a further nap (apparently in the bedroom)
and then toward afternoon's end, around 6 p.m.
was eager to head for the Ambassador Hotel in downtown LA.

Around 6:30 John Frankenheimer himself
drove RFK in his Rolls-Royce
                        to victory headquarters.

Apparently, Ethel was not quite ready,
and went to the hotel a bit later.

The children were to be transported to a bungalow at the
                        Beverly Hills Hotel.

The Agitated Drive to Downtown LA

Frankenheimer wheeled his Rolls-Royce Silver Cloud
along the Pacific Coast Highway from Malibu,
then rather rapidly
      on the Santa Monica Freeway.

Since the last week of March, Frankenheimer had
shot thousands of feet of film
      to help Kennedy win in the fall.

Kaiser's description, from Frankenheimer, has it that RFK
had been edgy that evening, unable to sit still during supper,
preoccupied about the outcome of the California primary.

Frankenheimer missed the Vermont off-ramp, "and got tangled up
      in the Harbor Freeway interchange."
          He cursed angrily as he tried to get the Rolls
          headed back toward the Ambassador.

"Take it easy, John," said Bob Kennedy. . . . "Life is too short."

RFK was dropped at the hotel around 7:30.

Agitated Indeed

      He couldn't really rest
      till after the convention in Chicago,

      so much convincing, even wheedling
            and begging
               he & his team would
                  have to do,

      and then of course not much of a rest because
      the fall campaign against Richard Nixon,
      who seemed likely to prevail over Nelson Rockefeller
            then would loom.

So, no wonder RFK was agitated at the hotel.
A writer for *Look* magazine also noticed the agitation.
Had RFK maybe learned something?

His mind was long accustomed to
                    compartmentalizing information.

        Whatever the reason,
        whereas the ocean had fully restored his vim,
                    the uncertainty over the vote tally
                    compounded the agitation at the hotel.

Peter Smith, long-time key aide to RFK, told the FBI
that as the "favorable totals came in everybody
        became more jubilant and that as it became
        evident that Kennedy was going to be the winner
                    he, Kennedy, became
                    more relaxed and in better spirits
                    than he, Smith, had seen him
                            in many months."

        Smith said that in RFK's suite
        a small meeting of RFK and staff
        then decided to hold a press conference
                    for the pen-and-ink press
                    in the Colonial Room
                    after the victory speech.[109]

Kennedy's Suite at the Ambassador

        In the eager energy of the packed victory suite
        RFK had Hubert Humphrey on his mind,

        talking about making Humphrey debate him,
        how he was "going to chase his ass
                    all around the country."

Meanwhile in Room 511 Ethel had just arrived
        from a windswept day in Malibu
        so her hair was combed by a hairdresser named Terry Haker

(who had also combed and set her hair the morning before the
exhausting campaign trips of June 3).

Terry Haker told the FBI later "that at 8:30 a.m. on June
        3, 1968 she set and combed Mrs. Kennedy's hair
        in the latter's suite, number 511, and then departed.

"She advised that about 7 p.m. on June 4, 1968, she,
           Arlene and Mary went up to the room of Provi Parades
on the fifth floor of the Ambassador Hotel.

"She stated Miss Parades worked for Mrs. Kennedy and
was to pay her for working on Mrs. Kennedy's hair.
           She stated her girlfriends accompanied her
           in hopes of seeing Mrs. Kennedy and her late husband.
           She stated that she waited for about one-and-one-half hours
           and then got paid by Miss Parades,
                        who also gave her a photograph of Senator
                        Kennedy for Mrs. Kennedy to autograph.
           Miss Baker stated she waited in the hall of the fifth floor for
           about one half an hour and saw Mrs. Kennedy, who
           at that time asked her to again comb her hair.

"She stated she went to into Room 511 with her
and combed her hair.
           She said following this,
Mrs. Kennedy signed her husband's photograph
                        and after this, Miss Haker left."[110]

Party-Time Mood in the Hotel

A fairly huge encampment
of heavyweight supporters
                had gathered at the
                Ambassador Hotel
                        to salute RFK
                        & his ever-growing campaign—

writers, politicians, attorneys,
thinkers, stars & very dedicated supporters—

I would guess 2 or 3,000 strong
exulting &, frankly, partying

that night
especially jubilant in the Embassy Ballroom.

Young fellows in Kennedy strawhats
& women in white blouses,

Victory suite

red Kennedy sashes
and blue skirts.

The polls closed at 8
It became certain that
a huge Los Angeles pro-RFK vote
was surging him to Victory!

Shortly after 9, Senator George McGovern called with
good news from South Dakota.
Bobby had won with more votes than
Humphrey and McCarthy combined

A call came in from Richard Daley.
who would run the Democratic Convention in Chicago in August.
He was now an official RFK supporter.

Pierre Salinger was next to Kennedy
when Daley called:

"Bobby & I exchanged a look
that we both knew meant
only one thing—
he had the nomination."[III]

A Conversation about *The Manchurian Candidate* in Suite 516

Writer Pete Hamill was on hand in Suite 516
with its tall windows overlooking Wilshire Boulevard
drifting in the foggy night.

Hamill later wrote: "While we waited in 516 for the polls to close
and the returns to come in, I talked for a while with the movie
director John Frankenheimer. The advertising agency Papert, Koenig, Lois,
Inc., had hired him in March to work with the Kennedy campaign
on promotional material, including some commercials.

"We talked . . . about Frankenheimer's great paranoid masterwork
from 1962, *The Manchurian Candidate,* which starred Frank Sinatra and
Laurence Harvey. It had been withdrawn from public viewing
after the killing of Jack Kennedy in 1963 (it would be re-released

in 1988). There was a decent reason behind the movie's
disappearance. The story, based on a novel by Richard Condon,
was about programming a man to assassinate a
                           presidential candidate.

"'Do you think it could happen in what is laughingly
called 'real life'?' I asked Frankenheimer.

"He smiled in a nervous way, and glanced at the door of the
suite. 'Yeah.'" [112]

> —from *A Time It Was: Bobby Kennedy in the Sixties*,
> photographs and text by Bill Eppridge,
> essay by Pete Hamill, Abrams, New York

Sirhan on Primary Day

Election day Sirhan
—as we have traced—had planned to go to
Hollywood Park for the horse races.

Sirhan said he checked the lists of races in the newspaper
and gave up after not liking the horses that were running.

More on Sirhan Sirhan Target Shooting

As we have noted, three days previous to election day,
on Saturday, June 1,
24-year-old Sirhan Sirhan had gone to the
                           Corona Police Firing Range
in the company of a man who fit the description
of the man with the foreign accent and turned-down mustache
who had worked on his mind in a prison-like hospital
                   where he had spent two weeks or so
                   after his fall from a horse in September 1966.

On June 1 at the Corona Police Firing Range
Sirhan later recalled that the range master showed him
how to shoot at human targets and vital organs.

Then, on the afternoon of June 4th, while the polls
were still open for the primary,
                    Sirhan went target shooting at the same time as
                    a pretty young woman, & interacted with her,
                    quick-firing 300 to 400 rounds
with a .22 at the San Gabriel Valley Gun Club in Duarte, outside LA.

Witness Recalls Sirhan Firing Quickly
and from a Crouching Position

James Thornburgh was interviewed by the FBI
He arrived at the gun range 10:30 to 11:00 a.m.
to practice with his new Ruger automatic .22 pistol.

He set up in the pistol range and noticed a young man
            he ID'ed as Sirhan Sirhan firing to his left.
"Thornburgh stated that he left the range at approximately
            2 p.m. and to the best of his knowledge, Sirhan had left
                    the range sometime between 12 p.m. and 1 p.m."

"Thornburgh stated that one thing that sticks
in his mind concerning Sirhan was the fact that he was
            shooting more rapidly than others on the range
and the fact that he was shooting from a
            rather unusual crouching position."[113]

            Then Sirhan drove away,
            ultimately winding up in Pasadena
                        in the late afternoon.

FBI States Sirhan 11 a.m.–ca. 3 p.m.
at Shooting Range

Sirhan "at San Gabriel Valley Gun Club from approximately
11:00 a.m. to 3 p.m. Bob's Restaurant, Colorado (Blvd) and
Pasadena City College Cafeteria about 6:00 p.m.–7:15 p.m."

            Question: what did he do between
            3 p.m. and 6 p.m.?[114]

Sirhan to Pasadena City College
Afternoon–Early Evening after Target
Shooting June 4, 1968

"Gaymoard Mistri advised that he came to the United States
from Bombay, India, five years ago. He related that
he attended Pasadena City College (PCC), Pasadena, California,
for two years, after which he transferred to the Western State College
of Engineering (WSC) at Englewood, California.
He studied there for two years and was graduated one week ago
with a degree in Engineering. Gaymoard Mistri explained
that he is presently unemployed and in the process of seeking a job
after obtaining his degree.

"He thereafter furnished information as follows:

"In 1962 or 1963, Mistri was attending PCC and belonged
to a social club called the Foreign Student's Group.
This club was for all foreign students on campus.
Through the club, he developed speaking acquaintances
with various other foreign students, one of whom was Sirhan Sirhan. . . .

"Mistri further explained that he continued to reside
in Pasadena while attending WSC and would often eat
        or attend social functions on campus at PCC.
        On some occasions, he would see Sirhan
        but estimates that in the last three years
                he has not seen him over four or five times. . . .

"On June 4, 1968, at approximately 6:10 p.m.,
Mistri entered Bob's Big Boy Restaurant,
                1616 East Colorado Boulevard, Pasadena.
The restaurant is adjacent to the campus at PCC.
Mistri sat at the counter for approximately ten minutes
after which Sirhan entered the restaurant, recognized him
                        and joined him at the counter.

"After greeting him, Sirhan asked Mistri to join him for dinner
and stated, 'The meal is on me.' After Mistri declined the offer,
Sirhan took Mistri's check for coffee. After a few minutes of
non-specific conversation, Mistri began reading a newspaper
which carried a caption concerning the Israel-Jordan situation.

"Sirhan noted the caption and said words to the effect of
      'things are wrong there.'
However, Mistri did not pursue the conversation,
    and Sirhan made no further comments concerning
      Israel, Jordan, or any other political situation or figure.

"Sirhan's meal was served, and the remainder of the conversation
was of horse racing, about which both had a mutual interest.

"When Sirhan finished his meal and paid the checks,
he asked Mistri where he was going. When Mistri informed him
that he was going to the PCC campus, Sirhan stated,
          'I think I'll come with you.'

"They then walked to the campus cafeteria,
during which time they again talked of horse racing.
Upon entering the cafeteria, Sirhan observed four Arab students
whom he immediately approached. He introduced himself
and after which a conversation ensued in Arabic. Mistri
recognized one of the students to be_____ whose address Mistri
furnished from an address book as _____ He did not recognize
the other students. _____ and the other students then departed
the cafeteria to attend a 7:00 p.m. class,
        and Mistri and Sirhan sat at another table. . . .

"A casual and non-specific conversation then began,
during which time, Sirhan began toying with a small metal object
which he held in his hands. When Mistri asked what the object was,
Sirhan advised that it was something connected with a gun or bullet.

"Mistri explained that Sirhan told him what the object was
but noted that he cannot now recall exactly what the object was.
He noted, however, that he is sure that it was connected with guns
      or bullets and stated that his impression is
        that it was a spent slug of a bullet which had been fired
          from its casing and subsequently recovered. . . .

"After Mistri inquired about the above-mentioned object,
he asked Sirhan if he was a hunter. Sirhan replied that
he had hunted on occasion but noted that he was just learning
about the sport. However, Mistri noted that he then asked Sirhan
an unrecalled question about rabbit hunting and pointed out that,
judging from the conversation that followed,

he formed the opinion that Sirhan had little
or no knowledge about hunting or firearms.

"Shortly thereafter, they departed the cafeteria and began walking
to a campus parking lot where each had a car parked.
While walking toward the lot, Sirhan observed a new campus building
and noted that the new building stands on what was a vacant lot
when they attended PCC.

"Sirhan then, referring to the time when they attended PCC as
students,
said words to the effect of, 'That was a beautiful time.'
he felt that the statement was odd and did not exactly understand it;
however, inasmuch as he did not wish to continue the conversation,
he made no comment and neither did Sirhan.

"While walking toward the lot, they came to a newspaper rack,
from which Mistri purchased a Preview Edition
of the *Los Angeles Times*.
When Sirhan stated that he also wanted a paper,
Mistri told him not to purchase one inasmuch as he, Mistri,
wanted only the classified ad section section (sic) and
gave the remainder of the paper to Sirhan.
Mistri does not recall seeing Sirhan look at the paper.

"As they approached their vehicles in the parking lot,
Sirhan asked Mistri if he wanted to shoot pool.
After Mistri declined, Sirhan lingered for a few moments
talking about mutual friends. Mistri recalled that Sirhan
asked such questions as how former students were getting along
and how many children they now have.

"As they entered their respective vehicles, Mistri recognized
that Sirhan entered the same vehicle which he had
when they attended PCC. He described the vehicle as an older model
Chrysler product which was pink in color. Mistri departed
the lot first
and did not observe the direction in which Sirhan drove away.
Mistri estimated the time to be 7:15 to 7:30 p.m.

"Mistri could not recall the clothing worn by Sirhan, other than
he was not dressed in a coat or tie and wore shirt and trousers.

"Mistri concluded by noting Sirhan made no comment
about Senator Robert F. Kennedy,
	the current political situation,
		or the primary election being held in California.

"Further, he stated that Sirhan gave no indication
of emotional instability or any type of contemplated
			violent act.
Mistri further noted that when Sirhan asked him
to go shoot pool, there was no time limit suggested.
He further stated that it was his opinion
that Sirhan appeared to be lingering with nothing to do
and was seeking his company.

"He noted, however, that no time limit
was suggested about shooting pool,
		inasmuch as he refused Sirhan's offer outright."[115]

LA DA's Time Track on Sirhan during the Evening of June 4, 1968—A Confusing Time Line for Sirhan

The LA district attorney's time line has it that
after finishing his hours of shooting on the gun range,
Sirhan had dinner at Bob's Big Boy restaurant and observed a
newspaper ad which read,
		"Join in the miracle mile march, for Israel
		tomorrow, Wednesday, June 5, at 6 p.m.
		on Wilshire Boulevard."

Sirhan testified that "this advertisement brought him back to the
six days in June of the previous year, and that the fire started burning
			inside of him as a result of the ad."
			(info from reporter's transcript, Sirhan's trial, page 5,175)

"Sirhan mistakenly thought the parade was scheduled
for that evening, June 4, and set out to observe it.
He testified that he was driving like a maniac, got lost,
and eventually arrived at Wilshire Boulevard where he looked

for the parade.
The gun was still in the backseat.

(Sirhan parked his DeSoto in the 600 block of New Hampshire
Avenue south of Wilshire Blvd.)

Of course, the question remains why was Sirhan so intent
on attending this Miracle March for Israel? Which miraculously
brought him very close to
                the Ambassador Hotel.

"His wallet, he testified, was in the glove compartment,
as he always carried his loose money in his pocket
             and he never kept a wallet on his person.

     "When Sirhan saw a sign for
          United States Senator Kuchel's Headquarters,
     he stopped by and was told that a large party for
     Senator Kuchel was going on at the Ambassador Hotel.
     When Sirhan walked toward the hotel, with his gun still
           in the automobile, he observed a large sign
     concerning some Jewish organization and Sirhan testified
          that this 'boiled him up again.'

"Upon entering the lobby of the hotel, Sirhan observed a sign
at the entrance to the Rafferty Headquarters which was located
in the Venetian Room. Sirhan joined the Rafferty celebration
where he testified that he stayed an hour. Sirhan's main purpose
was to see Rafferty's daughter, whom he knew from high school,
but he never saw her that evening. While at the Rafferty party,
         he testified he ordered two Tom Collins drinks."[116]

Dr. Max Rafferty

Conservative Republican Rafferty defeated incumbant US Senator
Thomas Kuchel in the Republican primary that day
(but lost to Democrat Alan Cranston
              the coming fall).

    His campaign headquarters were at the Ambassador.

Two Guys Meeting Sirhan
at the Ambassador

Two gentlemen, Enrique Rabago & Humphrey Cordero,
drove to the Ambassador Hotel between 9 & 9:30
           to view the RFK festivities

Both were dressed in casual clothes
and therefore Rabago was hesitant to walk into
the main lobby, but did so, urged on by Cordero

There was a huge crowd and the two became separated &
Mr. Rabago returned to the "porch area" of the hotel's
                  main entrance
hoping to locate his friend.

There on the porch stood Sirhan Sirhan
               holding a drink
& Rabago spoke with Sirhan.

"Are we going to win?" Rabago asked him
and Sirhan answered, "I think we're going to win."
Rabago replied, "I don't know, McCarthy is ahead now."

According to Rabago to the FBI, Sirhan said,
"Don't worry about him if he doesn't win,
the son of a bitch, he is a millionaire and
            he doesn't need to win.

"He just wants to go to the White House
but even if he wins he's not going to do anything for
you or for me or for any of the poor people."

Rabago remarked to the FBI that Sirhan further remarked:
"Kennedy did not care about any poor people and merely
sought to gain the Presidency for personal reasons" and
that "Kennedy was going to buy the Presidency."

Rabago told the FBI that at this point he was disgusted
and about to leave the porch when his pal Cordero
located him, and said, "Let's go back into the lobby."

Rabago felt that his clothes were inadequate, but Cordero
said to Sirhan, "Look at my friend, he doesn't want to go
in because of his clothing. What do you think of that?"

Rabago stated that Sirhan replied, "We're voters.
    I can go in there like this.
    I just returned from the Rafferty headquarters."

Sirhan told Cordero that he had gone into Rafferty
  headquarters to order a drink, and those inside
  had stared at him and, in the FBI's words,
    "obviously disliked him because of his clothing."

"Rabago advised that he (Sirhan) continued by telling Cordero
that the 'big wheels' stared at him while he ordered a drink
from the hostess and that he 'showed them'
    by paying for his drink with a $20 bill
    & leaving the change for the hostess."

Then Rabago (and Cordero) walked toward the
    television monitor, and Sirhan
      slipped out of his ken.

(Rabago and Cordero volunteered to talk with the FBI
on June 5, same day as the shooting, and this account
  relies on the FBI typist for its flow.)[117]

    A waiter at the Ambassador named Gonzalo Cabrillo
    told the FBI that he went to the restroom
    behind the Venetian Room,

        where the Max Rafferty party
        was being held.

    Sirhan approached Cabrillo, and said he
    was tired and wanted to relax. Cabrillo
    held Sirhan's drink while Sirhan obtained
      a chair.

    Sirhan was holding folded or rolled newspapers
      under his left arm, according to Cabrillo.

    Then later, circa midnight Cabrillo saw

Sirhan standing in front of the ice machines
in the service pantry
where RFK wd soon be shot.

Sirhan, said Cabrillo, was still carrying newspapers
under his left arm.[118]

Returning to Automobile

Sirhan testified that he returned to his automobile
and "Couldn't picture myself driving my car at the time
in the condition I was in."
He feared receiving a traffic citation or having an accident
without being covered by insurance, and decided to return
to the party to sober up with some coffee.

"He testified that he did not remember picking up the gun
from the car seat before returning to the hotel for coffee,
but that he 'must have.' He states the next thing
he remembers was being choked and being brought
to a police car with a flashlight shone in his eyes."[119]

Dr. Daniel Brown's Report on
Hypnotizing Sirhan in Recent Years

In recent years, beginning in 2008, Sirhan was examined
and hypnotized for 60 hours over a three-year period, by a
Harvard University memory expert, Dr. Daniel Brown.
Half of the interviews involved hypnosis, and Dr. Brown has reported,
in a court filing in 2011, the following about Sirhan Sirhan's memories,
on what he did on June 4, 1968:

Gun Range then Arriving at Ambassador in Evening

"Mr. Sirhan freely recalled going to the gun range during the day
of the assassination." Sirhan claimed he arrived at the Ambassador
later that evening, looking for a party. Dr. Brown states that
Sirhan recalled: "Now I'm going to another area . . .

I don't know the name . . . Later I heard it was the Embassy Room . . .
it's like a huge hallway . . . tremendous lights . . . no tables . . .
the brightness . . . a lot of people . . . I'm getting tired . . .
I wasn't expecting this . . . It's getting hot . . . very hot . . .
I want to get a drink. A make-shift bar area . . . I see a bartender. . .
a white smock . . . he looked Latin . . . we just nodded . . .
I told him what I wanted . . . it's like I have a relationship with this
guy . . . Tom Collins . . . I drink it while I'm walking around . . . this
bartender . . . he wasn't looking for a sale . . . he wasn't talkative . . .
it is like he's communicating with gestures . . .

a nod after I paid for it.

"I'm still looking around . . . he didn't make it (the drink) right
in front of me . . . he made it and brought it over . . .
after that I came back again . . . it was like a routine between us . . .
like I'm more familiar . . . like I'm a regular customer of his . . .
I don't remember seeing him before . . . it seemed like he was a
professional . . . he never initiated a conversation but after a
second time it was like there was a communication between us . . .
he knew what I wanted . . . it's hard to figure out if he's targeting me
or I'm targeting him . . . I don't remember him saying anything
like 'shoot Kennedy' or anything like that . . . he's just very quiet . . .
I begin to get tired . . . I sat down on one of the couches . . .
I remember feeling that I had to go home . . very bright lights . . .
like under the sunlight . . . I want to go home . . . I've seen the party."

Dr. Brown: "It is notable that at this point in time Mr. Sirhan
can only think about going home. Again, his expressed desire to leave
the party and go home does not suggest the motivation of an assassin
ready to kill a presidential candidate shortly thereafter."

Sirhan Returns to His DeSoto

Sirhan did attempt to go home, according to Dr. Brown's report:
"I get in the car . . . I couldn't think about driving the car . . .
it was late . . . I sit in the car . . . I couldn't make myself
drive it . . . There was no way I could drive the car . . . I don't want to
chance it . . . I wanted to sleep . . . I wanted to sleep . . . sleep . . . sleep . . .
sleep. Then I go back to the hotel to get some coffee."

According to Brown, "Mr. Sirhan recalled re-tracing his steps to the same bar. When Mr. Sirhan arrived at the bar he asked the same bartender for coffee. The bartender told him that there was no coffee at the bar. An attractive woman with a polka-dot dress was sitting at the bar talking to the bartender. She over-heard Sirhan asking for coffee and she said that she knew where coffee was."

Sirhan does not recall bringing his .22 from his DeSoto into the hotel. Dr. Brown: "Mr. Sirhan is adamant in his belief that he never brought the gun into the Ambassador Hotel. When asked to explain how he might have gotten a gun, he recalled being bumped up against and pushed around in the crowd on his way back to the bar to get coffee. He speculated, without specific recall, that the gun might have been placed in his waist band without his knowing it.

It is also possible that the girl in the polka-dot dress handed him the gun, but he does not remember so."[120]

Pink & White DeSoto

Perhaps when Sirhan returned to his DeSoto
he was followed

& he was then escorted
back to the Ambassador
by the woman in the polka-dot dress
                    along with a male
& they all entered the hotel
up the fire escape steps
        past Sandra Serrano
        sitting on the steps.

The Delegate Situation

Hubert Humphrey announced he was running
in late April
        after Johnson had abdicated.

He picked up backing from labor unions
and other Democratic groups.

A Tom Collins at the bar

He did not enter the primaries
but focused on
getting commitments from delegates
in non-primary states,

while Humphrey stand-ins ran in certain states.

By the California primary
Hubert Humphrey
was ahead in committed delegates.

With a California victory
RFK had a good chance
to overtake the vp
on the issue of his support for the war.

(In the 1968 primaries
a. Lyndon B. Johnson won New Hampshire.
b. Eugene McCarthy had won Wisconsin & Oregon
and would go to win Illinois, Massachusetts, New Jersey,
and Pennsylvania.
c. Robert F. Kennedy won California, Indiana, Nebraska, DC
and South Dakota.
d. Stephen M. Young, as stand-in for Hubert Humphrey, won Ohio.
e. George Smathers, standing in for Humphrey, won Florida.)

RFK's Plans for the Next Several Days

He intended to rest 2-3 days in California
then head off to New York
in the struggle with Humphrey
for the June 18 primary.

Were Angry, Murder-Minded CIA Officers on Hand in the Embassy Room at the Ambassador Hotel Before and After the Shooting?

A few years ago a filmmaker named Shane O'Sullivan became interested in the killing, and put together a film titled *RFK Must Die* (not to be confused with Kaiser's book).

During his research Mr. O'Sullivan
viewed still photos (on microfilm) and films taken at the
Ambassador Hotel that fateful night

>and found images of three humans
>which at the time he was sure were key CIA mal-minds
>on hand in the Embassy Room
>before and just after the shooting:

>1. David Morales, a hefty CIA veteran
>>with a Touch of Evil to his demeanor
>>who apparently later on in 1973
>>bragged about being in Dallas during JFK
>>and also on hand for RFK:
>>"I was in Los Angeles when we got the little bastard."

>2. Gordon Campbell
>>a CIA officer

>3. George Joannides
>>a highly placed CIA snuff-oid

(Joannides was hauled out from retirement later (in 1978)
to serve as the CIA's liaison with the
>far-famed House Select Committee on Assassinations.)

More on CIA Agents Plus the Possibility of Additional Killers at the Ambassador?

Shane O'Sullivan in his RFK documentary
had filmed footage of former CIA officer Brad Ayers viewing
a twenty-minute film of footage taken that night
>at the Ambassador
>and assembled by LAPD

and Ayers identified a guy who was a CIA off-oid
named Gordon Campbell, who was walking with another
>guy through the crowd right around the time of the killing.
George Joannides ides
>a highly placed CIA snuff-oid

(Joannides was hauled out from retirement later (in 1978)
to serve as the CIA's liaison with the
		far-famed House Select Committee on Assassinations)

David Rabern

Ayers located for O'Sullivan another guy
named "David Rabern, Covert Operations Specialist,"
a CIA agent in LA in June of 1968
whom O'Sullivan interviews on videotape
		for his film on RFK.

Rabern lived near the Ambassador at the time of the assassination.
Rabern recalled on tape that a CIA guy suggested he be there on
election night.
		He was, and was leaving the hotel, after the speech, when
		he heard the faint
		popping sounds of the shooting.

O'Sullivan showed Rabern a picture of Campbell and Joannides,
and Rabern said he'd seen Campbell earlier that evening speaking with
Morales.

David Rabern speculated that he felt that there were probably more
than one
		armed assassin on hand in the hotel that night,
						prepared to kill RFK.

He spoke about camouflaged firearms, concealed in various ways,
such as in a purse,
		which could be "popped open" to reveal a firearm. Pop pop.

"Silencers can be made out of all kinds of things," said Mr. Rabern
"maybe a book or something like that."

You walk up, say, to someone in a busy airport.
"You pop them. Then you walk away
					in the other direction."

O'Sullivan asked Rabern if he could describe to O'Sullivan how he
knew Gordon Campbell. Rabern replied, after a slight pause, "No."

A touch of evil

Is Campbell still alive? asked the narrator.

Rabern: "To my knowledge, he is."[121]

Morales in Ballroom

Morales was seen standing in the back of the ballroom
in "news coverage" images
"in the moments between the end of" RFK's speech
and the shooting.

"Thirty minutes later," O'Sullivan has written, "there he was again,
casually floating around the darkened ballroom
while an associate with a pencil mustache took notes."

(Could the pencil-mustached guy
be the one mentioned by Sirhan Sirhan
as taking him to the police firing range
& conducting notebook-writing sessions
with him via shortwave radio?)

(Also, the possibility that the wide-bodied and hefty CIA
regime-toppler named David Morales was at the Ambassador
calls to mind an FBI interview with Juan Romero,
an employee in the Ambassador kitchen who had knelt above
the stricken Candidate by the ice machine:

"Approximately two days before the shooting occurred . . .
he (Romero) was working at the hotel when he was
approached by two white males. He recalls that one
of the white males was very stout. . . .
and approximately 45 years old. . . . The stout one talked to him
and asked him where he could get a hotel jacket similar
to the one Romero was wearing. He told Romero
that they were police officers, but Romero did not ask for
or see any identification.

"Romero reluctantly took these individuals down to the
supply room area, but when they arrived there, the
supply room was closed."[122]

218

Was the stout man Romero mentioned
David Morales? Or perhaps hefty CIA off-oid
William Harvey?

There has been controversy raised over the identification of
Gordon Campbell and George Joannides

with some respected researchers claiming—including O'Sullivan himself
who later changed his mind, and now apparently believing—
that Campbell & Joannides were instead likely executives with the
Bulova Watch Company staying at the Ambassador
        as part of a Bulova sales convention.
        although, as we have traced, several former colleagues
        identified Campbell, Joannides and Morales
        from television footage shot in the Embassy Ballroom
        around and after the shooting.

        The questions remain: were dire CIA snuff-oids
on hand at the Ambassador
        at the moment the Senator was hit?

        Especially David Morales,
        a CIA hitman

E. Howard Hunt told his son not long before his passing that
he had attended a gathering
in 1963 in Miami at a CIA safe house invited by Frank Sturgis.

Also at the meeting was David Morales
        nicknamed El Indio
        & also nicknamed Didi.

"When some asshole needed to be killed, Didi was the man to do it,"
        commented a childhood friend of Morales
        speaking to writer David Talbot.[123]

Morales was in on the JFK hit:
"We took care of that son of a bitch, didn't we?"
        Morales stated to his attorney in 1973
        after a night of drinking.[124]

William Harvey, sent to be station chief in Rome by RFK,
was, according to Hunt, a leader of the plot.

David Morales said that Lyndon Johnson himself
          had signed off on the murd.

      Morales, apparently stationed in Laos, nominally, in June of '68,
      later bragged about being at the Ambassador on 6-4.[125]

Writer/filmmaker Shane O'Sullivan
described how one night in DC in '73
Morales childhood pal and Morales's attorney Robert Walton
were drinking. Walton described how Morales
became very upset in DC in '73 when the matter of JFK
came up. Walton: "He was striding around the room and he
was out of control," said Walton. "Morales said, 'I was in Dallas
when we got that motherfucker.

      'I was in Los Angeles when we got the little bastard.'"

Kennedy and the Kitchen Route

      As we have noted, the candidate tended
      to use back elevators and then a path through the kitchen
                to the hotel ballrooms for speeches.

      In Oregon he used the kitchen path, and
      at the hotel in San Diego, a freight elevator,

so Sirhan's handlers knew well before the night of fate
that since the target would come down the freight elevator
& through the kitchen
          to the Ambassador Ballroom,
          he'd likely go back out that way.

The Ambassador, with 600 rooms,
          had plenty of space
                    for a support team

      to work on an assassination.

**The kitchen route—Kennedy's final autograph
going into his final speech**

RFK's Route to and from His Victory Speech Was Supposed to Be Changed to Avoid the Kitchen

Pierre Salinger had been President John Kennedy's press secretary
and very prominent in the RFK campaign.
He was in charge of compiling the voter tally
                    for the press at each primary.

In his book, *P.S.: A Memoir*, Salinger described
how during the Oregon primary campaign
          he had spoken with campaign official Jim McManus,
          who had been involved beginning with the Indiana primary.

          "I had just instructed McManus to go
          to the Ambassador, the Los Angeles hotel where we hoped
          and prayed we'd be having our election night victory
          celebration, when he made a suggestion. He said he thought
          it would be a good idea if we kept the candidate
                    'out of the kitchen.'

          "Instantly, I knew what he meant. I recalled the chaotic
          scene at the hotel we'd used for the same purpose
          in Indianapolis. There's been a potential accident
          or mishap behind every corner on the route through
          the kitchen of that hotel—boiling water and greasy,
          wet floors. It made good sense to see if we could
          find a safer way to accomplish taking him past the
          public. I congratulated Jim, and told him
                    to implement his idea."

As it turned out, "a different coworker went to LA to check
out a safer route within the Ambassador Hotel. When he
got back, he verified that it was a good idea to use a different
route, and as he described the one he'd found, McManus, whose
idea it had been, sketched out the plan on a piece of brown
paper he'd torn off a lunch bag.

"Early the following morning, knowing I was to see Bobby
later in the day, Jim brought me the 'map.' I stuffed it in my
pocket, promising that I would give it to the senator.

"Later, when I saw Bobby in the suite at the Ambassador,
where he and Ethel were staying, we covered almost all
of the items on my mental checklist. One of those I didn't
get to was the plan for a new route through the bowels
of the hotel. . . .

"The next time I spoke to Jim it was 4:30 in the morning on
June 5. I'd called his hotel room in New York—where he'd gone
to set up shop for the press during the national campaign—
to tell him that Bobby had just been shot. . . .

"When he found his voice he asked me where it had happened, and
I said, 'in the kitchen.'

"'The kitchen!' McManus screamed at me, 'What the hell
was he doing in the kitchen?'

"All I could say was, 'I don't know.'[126]

—Pierre Salinger, *P.S.: A Memoir*, pages 198–199

Way Above Fire Code

The crowd was up to maybe 1,800 in the Embassy Room,
way above fire code,
　　　　　and it was very, very warm.

The overflow went down one floor
　　　　　to the Ambassador Ballroom.

One thing the thousands of pages of FBI RFK assassination files reveal
　　　　was how many film crews
　　　　　　from around the world
　　　　were positioned in the victory room.

I figure the killers maybe
　　　　had a TV or media team in the ballroom
　　　　　　with walkie-talkie or radio earpiece contact
　　　　　　with Sirhan's babysitters

(Recall the assertion that Army personnel
were taking pictures from a nearby roof

before and during the moments that Martin Luther King was shot.)

All the film and TV crews that were listed
                    in the FBI RFK "Kensalt" investigation files

makes me wonder if the kill team
did not actually at least film the stage
while they kept their eyes on it

—if only to radio the kitchen
that Kennedy was on his way.)

More Than One Robo-Programmed
to Help Kill RFK?

It's indeed possible that more than one person was
programmed to act under hypnotic suggestion.

> Don't scoff!
> Robotech is robotech
> & likely much more perfected in 1968
> 14 years after the experiments of 1954.

Is it possible that the robo-doctors got their hands on
Mr. Cesar, the security guard escorting Kennedy at the end?
And maybe even one or two members
of Kennedy's entourage

or even a staff person at the hotel

> to help steer Kennedy
> toward the Fatal & Unguarded Death-Trough?

(Indeed, Theodore Charach, creator of the film, *The Second Gun*,
in a press conference in 1995 stated that he believes
that Thane Eugene Cesar shot RFK in the head
but was programmed so that, like Sirhan,
            he has no memory of the shooting.)[127]

(Back in 1971, Mr. Charach filmed an interview with
Don Schulman, at the time of the assassination
            a runner with LA tv station KNXT.

It contained the following colloquy:
"Now, how far was Sirhan from Senator Kennedy at the time?"
Schulman: "I would say approximately from three to six feet."
"Where was this guard who was firing his gun?"
"He was standing directly to the side and back of Kennedy."
"On what side?"
"He was standing on the right-hand side. . . . I didn't see
everything that happened that night because of the blinding
lights and the people screaming, but the things that I did see,
I'm sure about. And that is, Kennedy being shot three times;
the guard definitely pulled out his gun and fired.)"[128]

Hypnotism expert Dr. Herbert Spiegel
gave the excellent researchers Jonn Christian and William Turner
a lead on robo:
Anything mentioned in the presence of a subject
under hypnosis is automatically etched into his mind
especially if it comes from the hypnotist,
and it might flow out at any time

I think that the intelligence agency robot-makers
had public interfaces, through doctors
and probably some hypnotists in LA, who

recruited victims
did background checks
then did their work on them
preparing them to kill.

Sirhan
was unable to recall anything about the assassination
during a 3-hr meeting
with Kenneth Hahn and LA-elected Supervisor Baxter Ward
at Soledad Prison
on June 2, 1977.

"I can't remember. I can't remember," he said
when asked about motive and if anybody else were involved.

"It's a blank."

Sirhan Recalling the Woman in the Polka-Dot Dress

"He remembered going to the hotel, he said, but not necessarily because Kennedy would be there. The night was still a jumble of twisted images. There was the meeting with the girl in the polka-dot dress whose name he never knew.

"'I met the girl and had coffee with
her,' he recounted. 'She wanted heavy on the cream and sugar.

"'After that I don't remember a thing
until they pounced on me in that pantry.'"[129]

Sirhan Staring by the Teletype

About 10:30, a Western Union teletype operator
noticed that Sirhan had come over to
her machine and stood there staring at it
She asked him what he wanted.
   He didn't answer, just kept staring
She asked him again.
   He just kept staring.
She said that if he wanted the latest figures on Kennedy,
he'd have to look at the other machine.
   He just kept staring.

Sandra Serrano and the Woman
in the Polka-Dot Dress
11:30 p.m.

A key-punch operator named Sandra Serrano had chaired the
Pasadena-Altadena area Youth For Kennedy Committee

and had come to the Ambassador to celebrate

but, because of the heat, left the crowded ballroom
  to sit outside on an exit stairway. It was about 11:30 p.m.

  Three people came up the stairway past her,
  a woman in a polka-dot dress

and two men,
one of them she later recognized as Sirhan Sirhan.

She remained on the stairway, she said, about another 1/2 hour

(note later in this poem how Polka-dot
raced back down these same steps
right after the assassination).[130]

John Justice Recalls Polka-Dot in the Serving Area

John Justice worked on the staff of RFK in the LA area.

On 6-4-68 Justice was in the serving area of the
Embassy Ballroom
"adjacent to the back right of the podium
helping one Rick Rosen keep people from
going into the serving area
from the Embassy Room.

"Sometime between 10:00 and 11:00 p.m. on June 4, 1968
Justice observed a man and a woman in the serving area
who, according to Justice, were 'definitely together,' and this
couple looked suspicious.

"Justice related that he asked this man to clear the area
and the man said he was from CBS. He was then asked
if he was with the camera crew and this man said, 'Yes.'
According to Justice, members of the press were supposed
to have a yellow press badge in their possession but that
neither one of this couple had such a badge visible
and Justice did not ask this couple to display a press badge.

"According to Justice, while this couple was in the
serving area the man made a phone call which was about
15 minutes in length, and after completing this call the
couple disappeared through the serving area and
this was the last time that Justice had seen him."

Justice's description: male, 5 feet 11; late 20s, light coat, dark pants. Female, "Attractive," late 20s, hair: "short, dark," dress: "Well-dressed with white dress having black polka dots."[131]

Walkie-Talkie Outside the Door

Outside RFK's door at the hotel
were plenty of reporters
plus a woman with a walkie-talkie,
          for instance

so that a spotter for the kill team
          could have easily been there unnoticed.

RFK went down one flight to
          speak with NBC
then back up to do the same with CBS,
          then ABC, then Metromedia.

He was pitching McCarthy and his supporters
          to join him to deny Humphrey the
               nomination.

Though important, California was not the final contest
          so now it was a matter of phone-power,
       mystique, twisting local Dems
              & jostling the War Caste.

The Kennedy Suite toward Midnight

The Kennedy Suite toward midnight
was packed with favored friends & campaigners

Just before going down to the ballroom,
speaking with close assistant Richard Goodwin,

       he whispered that he thought
       they should tell Senator McCarthy
       if he should withdraw and support him
       "I'll make him secretary of state."

In the final minutes in his suite
he chatted with Budd Schulberg
and some of his staff
on what to say
in his victory speech.

Then Kennedy was speaking with Civil Rights hero John Lewis:
"Wait for me," Kennedy said to Lewis,
"I'll be back in fifteen or twenty minutes."

To John Lewis, RFK looked so happy:
"he could have floated out of the room"

(An attorney named Anthony Akers, former ambassador
to New Zealand, was a key aide to the campaign,
and when RFK decided it was time
to go downstairs, Akers checked on the routine
to follow to get the Senator downstairs
and to the podium,
and as a FBI report states: "they took an elevator
to the basement of the hotel, walked
through a passage way to a freight elevator and up the
freight elevator to the floor wherein the ballroom and
podium were located. As far as Akers
can recall they entered the serving kitchen from the
freight elevator, walked by the serving table and ice machine
on up to the Podium. In the area of
the serving kitchen Robert Kennedy
shook hands with a few of the hotel employees."

As he led RFK to the victory podium,
Akers told the candidate that after his speech,
in the words of the FBI report,
"that he was going to clear a path so that when he (Kennedy) left the Podium
he could go to a ballroom on the floor below where there was a crowd of
people. He told Robert Kennedy to go to the left when he left the Podium
and Kennedy agreed to this."[132]

Cousin Polly Fitzgerald Spoke with RFK

For RFK in 1968, Polly Fitzgerald,
JFK's and RFK's cousin by marriage,

had organized the groups of young women
                on the Hostess Committee
She was at the Ambassador Hotel on June 4.

Just before going down for his acceptance speech,
Polly Fitzgerald later recalled, "He hugged me and we talked and I said,
'You're going to be president, and when you are, don't you forget the
middle-class people in this country in your zeal for the underprivileged,'
He said, 'I won't, I won't,' and he gave me a little hug and a kiss. He went
down to the ballrom and got shot."[133]

    RFK had a gulp of ginger ale
    Scanned himself in a mirror
    then he was urged to go down

    As he left, he asked that Al Lowenstein
                (organizer of the '67 Dump Johnson movement)
    be telephoned in New York
    to say that RFK'd call him
                right after the victory speech.

    RFK used the same path downward
                as back in Oregon
                    & recently in San Diego—
    down a hotel elevator, to the basement
    then up in a service elevator to the kitchen,
    & then through the kitchen and
    up to the stage for his victory speech.

    There was a sort of gridlock in the hallway
    outside the Kennedy suite
    headed for the elevators.

    He encountered his 11-year-old daughter Courtney
    and paused a couple of minutes asking her about what
    her day had been like.

    He stopped again for a brief chat with famous columnist
                Joseph Kraft,
    who had advised that RFK abandon the primaries & the campaign.

    He threw up a joke to Kennedy in the packed hallway,
    "Now you're trapped," meaning that with the California victory
    he would have to see it through to Chicago.

"You're going to be president."

Kennedy nodded and smiled,
then walked onward.

They went down a freight elevator
and through the kitchen,

then up an enclosed stairway
& onto the utterly packed stage
overlooking the overflowing Embassy Ballroom.

UAW Official Paul Schrade Recalls RFK Coming through the Double Swinging Doors from the Kitchen into the Ballroom to Give His Acceptance Speech:

"As we were walking through the kitchen
toward the Embassy Ballroom
it was one of those wonderful scenes.
The kitchen workers coming over to shake hands with him
and 'Viva Kennedy' and 'Kennedy for Presidente.'"

Kennedy walked onto the stage with Doris Huerta
[co-founder with César Chávez of the
National Farm Workers Association]
and escorted by Olympic decathlon champ Rafer Johnson
and pro football star Roosevelt Grier

plus of course Ethel and some of their children.
The applause and excitement was enormous
There were jubilant young men in Kennedy strawhats
& women in white blouses
red Kennedy sashes
& blue skirts

At first, there was trouble with the microphones on stage
which after about 20–30 seconds was taken care of
and wow was the stage crowded!

It was a time of playful joy.
The winner first congratulated
Don Drysdale of the Dodgers
who'd just won a 3-hit shutout.

"Now you're trapped."

"He pitched his sixth straight shutout tonight,
and I hope we have as good fortune
                    in our campaign."

He thanked those who'd helped him.
It was very, very hot in the ballroom.

The speech would run around 12 1/2 minutes,
well enough time
                    to place the robo-array
                                into position.

Too Close to Ethel

The 3-months pregnant Ethel Kennedy
was given security protection
during the speech

She was resplendent in what one biographer
described as
a sleeveless orange-and-white Courreges minidress,
with horizontal stripes above the midriff,
large circles below, with white stockings.

On the platform
Ronald Bennett
was taking pictures
—the area was shovy-packed,
and his camera, in the crush,
kept pushing against Ethel;

She complained
(Bennett was situated
right behind her).

"Rosey Grier grabbed him
from behind, placing
one hand around his stomach,
so as to prevent him
from being pushed into Mrs. Kennedy."[134]

Victory

Frankenheimer Watching on TV Monitor

After John Frankenheimer had driven Kennedy to the Ambassador,
as he later told an interviewer,
"I was supposed to be the guy standing next to Bobby on the podium."

Instead, the filmmaker decided to watch the speech on a tv monitor
"in the archway." As he was watching, he believed he perceived
Sirhan Sirhan brushing past him. "It was like *Manchurian Candidate*.
I felt this shaking inside of me."

Just before the shooting, Frankenheimer told the interviewer he
returned to his Rolls to await the candidate, and heard the
horrid news over the car radio.

Waiting with Frankenheimer was his wife Evans
They were going to drive Ethel and Robert
to the victory celebration at The Factory discotheque.[135]

Pierre Salinger during the Final Speech

While RFK spoke, "I began to think about the plans for the rest
of the evening. I was hosting a big victory party at The Factory,
a new Los Angeles discotheque of which I was part owner, along
with Paul Newman, Peter Lawford, and Sammy Davis, Jr." (The latter
was scheduled to perform at the party.)

The Path RFK Was Supposed to
Take after the Speech

He was supposed to walk down the steps
off the left side of the stage
and down through an enclosed stairway
to address the crowd in the Ambassador Room
below

The FBI interviewed William F. Gardner, chief security officer
at the Ambassador Hotel, who awaited RFK with two security
guards at the bottom of the enclosed staircase
from the Embassy Ballroom down to the
Ambassador Room:

"Shortly after midnight, on June 5, 1968,
he (Gardner) was located in the foyer on the Ambassador
Room level just at the bottom of the inside staircase
which leads down from the level
where the Embassy Room is located."

With Mr. Gardner were two security guards.
A Kennedy aide had requested them to be there
because RFK and friends were to "come down
the enclosed stairway and go to the
Ambassador Room
to talk to the people located there."

Then RFK, after a short talk to the people
in the Ambassador Room, was to go out
a fire escape and leave the hotel.

(John and Evans Frankenheimer waited
in their car outside.)[136]

A Plan to Talk with Pencil Press—Fred Dutton Interrupts and Changes RFK's Stage-Exit Plan

The FBI interviewed Uno Timanson, Ambassador vp:
"After the Senator had completed his victory speech
in the Embassy Room, he was preparing to lead the Senator down
down to the Ambassador Room through the enclosed stairway. Just
before the the Senator's speech was completed, Fred Dutton, one of
the Senator's aides, asked Timanson if there were television sets in
the Ambassador Room, and Timanson told him there were. It was then
decided that the Senator would visit the Press Room to make a
press release. Timanson escorted the Senator and his party
through the hallway behind the Embassy Room and into the pantry
area."[137]

Did someone
suggest this new
route to Dutton?
If so, then

was that person
part of the
　　plot?

So, the decision was made by Kennedy's staff,
likely solely by Fred Dutton,
apparently on the moment
to do a session
　　with the pencil press
in the Colonial Room.

His security guys were prepared
to take him to the pencils
by sidesteps off the stage

Dutton Tells the FBI That RFK Did Not Know His Route Had Been Changed

Dutton told the FBI, according to the FBI report,
"Dutton stated he decided that upon the completion
of Senator Kennedy's victory talk, the Senator would
go to the Colonial Room where the press had gathered,
rather than go down to the lower ballroom. . . .

"Dutton said he did not tell Senator Kennedy that
he was to proceed to the Colonial Room, but believed
that Bill Barry had done so, as Barry was aware of the plan."[138]

Therefore, while Kennedy was standing at the dais to speak
Fred Dutton told Uno Timanson, an executive at the hotel,
that Kennedy would not be going down to
the Ambassador Ballroom one floor beneath the Embassy
where the overflow was watching RFK on television monitors.

(The official daily press schedule had indicated he would go
to the Ambassador Ballroom after his speech. Below is
part of the "Memo to the Press" listing the June 4 schedule
issued by Kennedy headquarters:

—from FBI RFK Kensalt report, page 806

"The Senator will go to the Colonial Room," Fred Dutton told Timanson,
"to have a session with the pencil press."[139]

> The hit-group likely had a person
> on hand, posing as security personnel,
> who would have learned the new plan for RFK
> after the speech

> and thus was able to maneuver Sirhan Sirhan
> into the shooting zone
> by the RFK path
> through the kitchen pantry.

(Hours later Fred Dutton was video-interviewed.
Dutton said, "While the Senator was speaking,
(Bill) Barry and I went to look to see what would be
the route to take him from the stage
to where he went next.
There was one possibility of his going off to the right
of the stage and down a flight of stairs to an
overflow crowd in a room on the next lower floor.
However, in order to avoid further crowd scenes
which we had in the Embassy Room . . .
and because we had a number of reporters waiting
to talk to him, we decided to take him . . . to a press room
adjoining the Embassy Room.

"Barry and I saw the Senator was speaking,
walked that route, through the hallway
where the shooting finally occurred.

239

Walked over, walked back very quickly. . . .
We came back and went up on the stage.")[140]

James Marooney Accompanied Dutton and Barry to the Colonial Room and back to the Embassy Room during RFK's Celebration Speech

"Prior to Senator Kennedy's speech, Marooney heard that Senator Kennedy, after his speech, was going to go to the room below the Embassy Room and make a second speech to the overflowing crowd. However, Marooney heard that before going to make the second speech, Senator Kennedy was going to go to the Colonial Room, which was being used as a press room, to talk to the working press.

"During Senator Kennedy's speech, Marooney saw Fred Dutton and Bill Barry leave the Embassy Room. Marooney went with them. They went to the Colonial Room and then back to the Embassy Room. Marooney is of the impression that Barry and Dutton were just looking to see where the Colonial Room was located.

(But I don't think they realized that Kennedy was going to
be beckoned after the speech to exit though a curtain at the stage's back.)[141]

Sirhan Taken by Polka-Dot to Anteroom by the Stage Where RFK Is Speaking

Harvard Professor Dr. Daniel Brown, in his report in 2011
on his 60 hours of interviewing and
hypnotizing Sirhan Sirhan, stated that Sirhan
was led to a room off the stage
while Kennedy was giving his 10-minute victory speech:

"The woman in the polka-dot dress then took Sirhan
by the hand and led him to the anteroom
behind the stage where Senator Kennedy was speaking."

There they found some coffee, at which point, Sirhan begins to feel attracted to her ("It was my job to woo her.")
when all of a sudden, according to Brown,

"they are interrupted by an official with a suit and clipboard.
This official tells them that they cannot stay in the anteroom
for security reasons, and the official then tells
the girl in the polka-dot dress to go to the kitchen."

Official with Suit and Clipboard Sends Sirhan and Polka-Dot from an Anteroom by the Stage to the Kitchen

Sirhan to Dr. Daniel Brown: "All of a sudden they tell us, we have to move.
This guy comes by wearing a suit . . . darkish hair . . . a big full face . . .
seems like he was in charge . . . he wasn't wearing any uniform . . . wearing
a suit . . .
she acknowledges his instruction . . . he motions towards the pantry.
The man said, 'You guys can go back in this room.' I followed her. She led . . .
I was a little like a puppy after her. I wanted to go back to the mariachi band...
but she went straight to the pantry area . . . with my being so attracted
to her I was just glued to her."

Sirhan was clueless, possibly drugged. "She" and the "official" led him to
the very
place that the assassination was to occur.[142]

RFK's victory speech was just long enough
to get the kill team surely in place.

The patsy, Mr. Sirhan by the tray stacker
with Polka-dot.
The actual killer
either waiting by the ramp
leading down to the kitchen/pantry swinging door

or waiting just inside.

Peter Smith Goes outside to Check to See If the RFK Motorcade Is in Place

Around the time RFK began his speech,
aide Peter Smith went downstairs
"to assure that the motorcade was in position

at the door. Smith explained that
it had been necessary for the Senator's party
to contract with the Riggs Funeral Home people
for them to furnish escort service for the Kennedy
party while they were in Los Angeles.

"He said that they did not have police escorts and adequate
police protection in Los Angeles that everyone was led to
believe that they were offered and that this was the reason
that they had engaged Riggs as escort service."

Smith checked on the motorcade, then returned
to the Press Room where he was told that
RFK would go to the Press Room for a news conference
"and then go through the kitchen and out to
the motorcade."[143]

Security Guard's Statement to FBI

Stanley Kawalec was a security guard for the Ambassador Hotel.
Mr. Kawalec told the FBI that "his station was in a hallway
which is located directly behind a small anteroom
which, in turn, is located directly behind the stage in
the Embassy Room"

on which stage RFK delivered his victory speech.

"Kawalec advised that as Senator Kennedy was completing
his speech, he was ordered by the Chief Security Officer,
Mr. William Gardner, to vacate the spot which he had
directly behind the stage and assume a position in the
Embassy kitchen area."

He was to control the crowd "and make a passageway
for Senator Kennedy through a side door of the
Embassy Room through the Embassy kitchen to the
Colonial Room where the Senator was to have a press
conference."

Kawalec placed himself at the end of a steam table
facing the Senator
when he heard shots,

"You guys can go back in this room."

saw Kennedy was hurt

and worked with two LA Firemen
                to keep onlookers away from
                        the fallen Senator.[144]

Ambassador Hotel Director of Security Was Told during RFK's Speech that RFK Would Exit to the Street at the Rear of the Hotel

William Gardner, Ambassador Hotel director
of security, told the FBI "that near the conclusion
of Senator Kennedy's speech and while he was
stationed in the rear hallway behind the Embassy
Room podium, a female member of the Kennedy
campaign staff informed him that the Senator
intended to leave by the rear steps of the hotel,
and she asked him to ensure that a pathway
could be made for the Senator's exit.

"He stated that he immediately contacted the
front doorman and determined that Kennedy's
limousine and police escort had been moved
to the rear of the Embassy Room. He stated that
in view of these instructions he merely assumed
that Senator Kennedy would no longer greet
                the press in the Colonial Room."[145]

Thus the Chief of Security
was nowhere near RFK
                when he was shot

His Final Speech

After adjusting the microphones, and a fairly lengthy
list of those he thanked for their help,

Kennedy spoke for approximately ten minutes
(well enough time to get the robo-team in place).

After congratulating pitcher Don Drysdale
            for his sixth straight no-hit shutout,

the winner of California's 178 delegates,
relaxed and smiling,
            thanked his wife Ethel
            Rosey Grier, Rafer Johnson
                        (to great applause)
            and thanked the great support of
            Black voters, & the support of unions,
            specifically thanking the United Auto Workers'
            Paul Schrade
                        on the stage with him.

            He congratulated McCarthy.
            He pointed out that the
            "country wants to move in a different direction,
            we want to deal with our own problems
            within our country,
                        and we want peace in Vietnam."
                                    (great applause)
            He was looking forward to "a dialogue, or a debate,"
            with Humphrey
            "on what direction we want to go in; what we are
            going to do in the rural areas of our country, what we
            are going to do with those who still suffer
            within the United States from hunger . . . and whether
            we're going to continue the policies that have
            been so unsuccessful in Vietnam. . . ."

            Then he finished:
            "What I think is quite clear is that we can work together
            in the last analysis, and that what has been going
            on within the United States over the period
            of the past three years, the divisions,
            the violence, the disenchantment with our society—
            the divisions, whether it's between blacks and whites,
            between the poor and the more affluent,
            or between age groups, or on the war in
            Vietnam, that we can start to work together.

            "We are a great country,
                        an unselfish country,

a compassionate country,
and I intend to make
that my basis for running. . . .
　　(to great applause)

Then a spot of humor: "Mayor Yorty has just sent me a message,
that we've been here too long
already—so my thanks to all of you, and now it's on to Chicago,
and let's win there, thank you very much."

RFK flashed a brief V-sign with his hand then left the podium.

The crowd chanted
　　in a powerful rhythm
　　　　"We want Bobby, we want Bobby. . . ."

　　　　　　Behind RFK
　　　　　　the curtain
　　　　　　leading back
　　　　　　to the ramp
　　　　　　heading directly

　　　　　　to the killing zone

　　　　　　a voice:
　　　　　"This way, Mr. Kennedy."
　　　　　First rule:
　　　　　　　don't let yourself
　　　　　　　get peeled off from your guards.

His bodyguards
　　　Olympic hero Rafer Johnson
　　　and huge LA Rams tackle Roosevelt Grier
　　　started to help clear a path to Kennedy's left
　　　for RFK, Ethel, and the others

　　　down the steps

　　　There was a stairwell
　　　off to the side of
　　　　　the RFK podium
　　　　　　　leading down to the Ambassador Ballroom
　　　　　　　where RFK was

"We are a great country, an unselfish country,
a compassionate country."

scheduled to go next
      to speak with a second gathering.

Dutton had interrupted
that Flow
but without telling RFK's guards
      Rafer Johnson &
      Roosevelt Grier

that RFK would leave through the stage's back.

      So all three of the guards
      (including Bill Barry)
      prepared to clear a
      pathway
            for RFK, Ethel, et al.
            to proceed down the steps
                  stage right toward
                  the Colonial Room

      instead of the "enclosed stairway"
      leading to the downstairs ballroom
            RFK et al. were originally going to take.

Ambassador Executive Uno Timanson Tells of Change in Plans Given by Fred Dutton

      As we have indicated, Uno Timanson told the FBI
      the plan originally was for RFK to proceed
      to the Ambassador Ballroom below the Embassy
            to talk to his supporters
      but that, just before RFK concluded his speech,
      "Fred Dutton asked him if television sets had been
      set up in the Ambassador Ballroom and it was
      immediately following this, according to
      Timanson, that Dutton indicated the Senator
      would visit the Colonial Room, which was being
      used as a press headquarters.

      "Timanson had advised Dutton that television sets
      had been set up in the Ambassador Ballroom
      and Timanson is of the opinion that the Senator

possibly was going to skip going to the
Ambassador Ballroom.

"Timanson stated that he left the podium
to go to the Colonial Room and observed
there were no press representatives there and
that only four or five people were in the room
working at the teletype machine and apparently
compiling election returns.

"Timanson advised that he told Mr. Dutton of the
absence of the press and that the press was located
in the Embassy Room, but in spite of this
the Senator and his party, on leaving the stage,
proceeded through the Embassy kitchen area
in the direction of the Colonial Room.[146]

Political Power Jesse Unruh

had already spoken to the gathering in the Embassy Room
and then was on the stage when RFK spoke.

After the speech, Unruh told the FBI, RFK "started
to walk away. He proceeded to his right, toward
a table where Pierre Salinger and Dick Kline were seated.

"He (RFK) was propelled, by someone he could not see,
toward the back of the stage."[147]

RFK Guard, Pro Footballer Roosevelt Grier

Grier arrived at the Ambassador Hotel around 7:30 p.m.
6-4-68, and went directly to the coffee shop.
"Around 8:00 p.m. he observed Senator Robert Kennedy walk
past the coffee shop followed by his wife Ethel and other
unrecalled individuals."

Ethel spotted Rosey and invited him to their suite on the 5th
floor. First Grier went to the press room where he gave
press interviews. . . . "Grier spoke to Senator Kennedy about
the California primary election returns and relayed a message

from Pierre Salinger who requested he tell Kennedy
that he was leading with 50 percent of the votes returned
to San Francisco. . . .
Grier next accompanied RFK from the fifth to the
fourth floor to do two or three television interviews.

Bill Barry requested that Grier escort Ethel Kennedy.
They went down in a freight elevator, and departed the
elevator via a kitchen or serving area.

> "While Senator Kennedy was speaking, Bill Barry
> or Fred Dutton . . . told Grier that Senator Kennedy
> would be escorted from the stage from the left side
> since preparations had been made for his movement
> through the crowd. When Senator Kennedy finished
> speaking . . . Barry and Grier positioned themselves
> alongside of him.

> "Everyone on stage was aware the speech had ended
> and the crowd began to move toward the left.

> "Grier told Barry that the exit would be
> from the left side of the stage and Barry said 'ho.'

> Grier told the FBI "At this time Senator Kennedy
> moved to the rear of the stage possibly at Barry's
> suggestion and jumped to the floor.

> "…Grier assisted Mrs. Kennedy to the floor.… Grier could
> not see Senator Kennedy at this time but since
> the crowd was moving in that direction he assumed
> Senator Kennedy was in front of him. Grier
> was walking with Mrs. Kennedy and acting
> as her escort."

> Grier said he was about 10 or 15 feet into the kitchen
> area when he heard sounds like firecrackers. He
> saw an "individual holding a black object in his
> right hand which resembled a gun. This man
> held this object at waist level, his elbow was bent
> and his forearm was parallel to the floor. This man
> was standing on the floor."

Grier made his way toward the man with a gun.
Two other men, including Bill Barry, were wrestling
with the gun holder, pushing him back down upon
a "raised counter or table." Grier saw the gun knocked
from the gunman's hand onto the table, but then the
    gunman
retrieved the weapon. George Plimpton, Barry and others
were struggling to get the gun. Grier "placed his
own hand over the hammer and around the trigger
housing. He twisted the gun from his hand and gained
possession of the weapon."

Not long thereafter Grier gave the .22 to Rafer Johnson.
Grier said he'd not seen anyone run from the
    serving area after the shots,
    nor did he recall a woman wearing
    a white dress with black polka dots.[148]

Pierre Salinger Wanted RFK to Head Stage Right

Nina Rhodes was a volunteer fundraiser for RFK
who followed the results with Pierre Salinger,
Frank Mankiewicz and other staff members

Rhodes told the FBI:
"Approximately 15 minutes before his speech ended . . .
a tall blond man, name unknown, came over to the press
area (located in the Embassy Ballroom next to the stage)
and asked Pierre Salinger which way he wanted the Senator
to leave the stage. Salinger indicated that he wanted the
Senator to turn to his right, proceed through the
staff press area, then through the kitchen area to the
Colonial Room, the site of the main Kennedy press room. . . .
The Senator did not take the indicated route,
however, but exited the podium back through the curtains
to the rear of the stage which led to the
                    kitchen passageway."

Nina Rhodes watched the victory speech from the "press
    room area" to the left facing the stage.

Nina Rhodes previously had asked "Mr. Salinger
if she could personally congratulate the Senator when
he finished his speech and Mr. Salinger stated she could.

"The Senator did not take the indicated route, however,
but exited the podium back through the curtains
                    to the rear of the stage. . . .

"When this happened, Mr. Salinger said 'Go, baby'
indicating that she should follow the senator
quickly through the kitchen passageway.

"She grabbed Lucy Salinger's hand . . . and together they
                    ran into the kitchen passageway.
                    She stated this area slanted downward
                    in the direction they were running
                    and that it was cluttered
                        with all sorts of cables.

"She tried to focus her attention on the Senator's head,
thereby making it easier to determine his whereabouts.

"She had just left the entrance to the kitchen
and noticed the Senator shaking hands with various
kitchen employees and continue proceeding down the hallway
when she suddenly heard a sound like a firecracker
and she saw a red-like flash three to four feet
                    from the Senator's head."

Nina Rhodes fell to the floor, and misplaced her purse
Her husband soon helped her leave the area.

(See later on in this poem how Rhodes
claimed later she told the FBI she had heard
12–13 shots fired
            and not 8 as indicated in her 7-15-68 FBI report.)[149]

Assistant to Speaker of the California Assembly Recalls End of Speech

An assistant to California assembly speaker,
Jesse Unruh, stood at the foot of the stage
                    during the victory speech.

"Following the Senator's speech, the Senator proceeded
to walk to his right toward a table where
Pierre Salinger was seated, however
someone (unknown to him) but whom he believes
was in a tuxedo, pointed him in the
direction of the rear of the stage."[150]

(Gabor Kadar had a position on the right side
of the platform "because he noticed that
women dressed in Kennedy girl outfits
had formed an aisle for the Senator
to depart from the room.)

"When the Senator completed his speech
he did not come through the aisle
formed by the girls
but turned and walked off the back
of the stage and out through
the rear door."[151]

An assistant maître d' named Karl Uecker
parted the gold curtain
to the rear

and reached for Kennedy's arm
to lead him back through the curtain
off the platform's back.

While a voice urged, "This way, Mr. Kennedy."

Uecker turned Kennedy to his right
after passing through the curtain,
the Senator jumped down two feet
onto the regular stage
and through the anteroom
(from which Sirhan and the girl
in the polka-dot dress
had so recently been told
to leave and go to the kitchen pantry)

and then down an incline
toward the double door
which led to a service pantry and the kitchen.

Fred Dutton and RFK's main security guy Bill Barry
were caught off guard,
>thinking the Senator was leaving the
>stage the way he entered, down the
>>sidesteps.

>Barry told the FBI
>"that it was planned that Senator Kennedy
>would attend an official celebration party
>with volunteer workers of his campaign
>in the subbasement area
>>(the Ambassador Ballroom)
>after his victory speech.

>"After Senator Kennedy's victory speech,
>an unknown individual, possibly known to
>Fred Dutton, stated 'come this way'
>and directed the Senator toward the
>>kitchen hallway.

>"The Senator left the podium and departed the area
>by the rear exit behind the stage and approached
>a hallway as Barry assisted Mrs. Kennedy
>>from the podium.

>"Mrs. Kennedy told Barry 'to stay with the Senator.'. . .
>Barry fought his way through a dense crowd
>in an effort to circle the Senator's right flank and take
>his customary position immediately in front of
>Senator Kennedy. . . . As Barry was fighting his way
>through the crowd along the wall to the
>Senator's right and as he was directly opposite him,
>he heard a sound which resembled a firecracker."[152]

Though Bill Barry Thought RFK Was Leaving by the Side of the Stage, He Left through a Back Curtain

On the stage during RFK's speech was
William Eppridge, who told the FBI

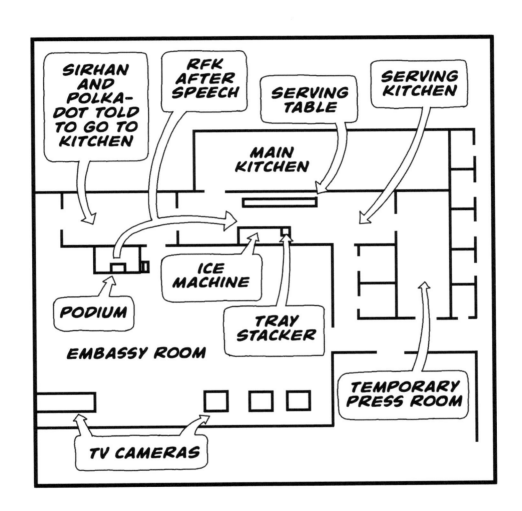

Kill Zone

that just before the end of the Victor's speech
a path was cleared off the stage and Bill Barry told RFK
        to go "this way" but RFK instead
    went out through a curtain at stage back.[153]

Forming an Aisle Leading from the Stage

Jane Kearns was employed in RFK's publicity dept.
She watched RFK give his speech
                in the Embassy Balloom
She told the FBI "that she and a number of other
campaign workers had spontaneously formed an aisle
or passageway through which they presumed
the Senator would walk through on his way out of
        the Embassy Ballroom."

            The passageway extended to the right
            of the podium toward an exit door.

"She said, however, that Senator Kennedy did not walk
toward the group-formed aisle but instead walked
            in the opposite direction
            toward the kitchen area."[154]

"Slow down!" someone cried.
"You're getting ahead of everyone!"
The bodyguards were
            not yet caught up.

The candidate was in effect alone
        Alone Alone
        w/ the excuse
            of Plot, Luck & Fate

(as we have noted, the hotel's chief of security
William Gardner, who had been guarding in
the hallway behind where RFK was
                delivering his speech
& thus was in a position
to guard the Senator when he left the podium,
had been called away during the speech
by a person who asked Gardner

256

to go to the rear of the hotel to set up a pathway
for RFK's departure from the hotel
        & was no longer vouchsafing him).

Uno Timanson was about 6 feet ahead of the Senator
when he heard the pops.
        He rushed to the outside of the hotel to wait for the
ambulance. He brought the ambulance attendants to where
RFK lay by the ice machine.

        (Also escorting the Winner
was a security guard named Thane Eugene Cesar. It's
not known if Cesar instructed Uecker to
                pull Kennedy back through
                the curtain and down the incline
                toward the swinging doors of the pantry.)

        It was hasty

        (Viewing the videotape of the speech &
                aftermath
there was just 2 and 1/2 minutes between
the Senator leaving the stage
and the flow of screams, shouts
        & consternation from the audience.)

George Plimpton and his wife Freddy
were on the platform with RFK
& followed him through the back curtains.

        Plimpton, anticipating that Senator Kennedy was
        going out the back of the stage, preceded Senator
        Kennedy and went to the right after leaving the stage.

        Plimpton told the FBI he "was walking along about
        12 feet in front of Senator Kennedy and would look
        back to see that he, Plimpton, was going
                in the correct direction. . . .

        "Senator Kennedy was about 12 feet
        behind him and was shaking hands with one of the
        kitchen employees. . . .

"He then looked forward and at that time
and heard very sharp shots. . . . and thinks that
there were five of them
in very rapid succession."[155]

RFK Practice of Shaking Hands
with Kitchen Workers

RFK sometimes visited kitchens and shook hands with staff,
such as on February 22, 1962 when RFK visited
the kitchen to thank the food preparers
after a banquet in his and Ethel's honor
in Berlin hosted by Mayor Willy Brandt.

Six years later he was still doing it,
greeting food staff
passing through the kitchen pantry after his speech.

Maybe the fact he tended to greet kitchen workers
was noted on 1962 intelligence reports
and proved useful in '68

when RFK unguarded by bodyguards
paused in the pantry.[156]

—page 204, Susie Wilson,
Still Running: A Memoir
(section, "Travels with the Kennedys")

Photographer Bill Eppridge Taking
Pictures for *Life* Magazine

Bill Eppridge was part of the RFK campaign from "one week
after Senator Robert Kennedy instituted his campaign to seek
the Democratic Party Presidential nomination."

Eppridge noted that RFK took
a service elevator to the ballroom to give
his victory speech.

**Shaking Vesta Morello's hand going through the kitchen
to his final speech**

"Shortly after getting off the elevator,
Senator Kennedy got out of line
and went into the kitchen of the hotel
and shook hands with some of the employees
in the kitchen.

"Senator Kennedy then got back in line and
proceeded along a corridor . . . and up the steps
to the platform.

Eppridge was on the speech platform, standing right behind
RFK and to the side.

"On the platform, there was a very large crowd, the largest
of the campaign and there was much shoving from behind
and the crush was so great that Eppridge could just barely
get his arms above his head."

"Immediately prior to Senator Kennedy ending his speech
someone opened a path to Senator Kennedy's right,
off the platform,
in what was apparently a route of exit
for Senator Kennedy.

"Bill Barry, a member of Senator Kennedy's staff,
was to the right and apparently leading the way to the path
and was telling Senator Kennedy to go that way.

"Eppridge did not hear Senator Kennedy's reply
if there was one,
but Barry again told Senator Kennedy
to go 'this way'
which was to Senator Kennedy's right.

Eppridge did not hear Senator Kennedy's reply
if there was one, but Senator Kennedy did not go
in the direction of Barry.
Senator Kennedy went through a curtain
out the back of the platform
and off the platform.

Eppridge does not know where Senator Kennedy was going
at this point. Eppridge was about 12 to 15 feet behind
Senator Kennedy.[157]

Photographer Bill Eppridge Recalls the Shots

"After getting off the back of the platform
Senator Kennedy went to the right. Eppridge was
following and when Eppridge got to some doors that seemed
small for the crowd he heard two shots in very rapid succession.
Eppridge at first thought these were fireworks as they
had been in Chinatown, San Francisco, the day before
and there were many fireworks there.

"There was a pause after the second shot and people
were scattering. Eppridge realized that what he
thought were fireworks were actually shots.

"He ran forward instinctively thinking he had better
count the shots. He counted a total of six shots.

"As he was running forward there was screaming and
bedlam. He then saw a man lying on the floor. He took
three pictures of this individual who at first
he thought was Bill Barry. It was Paul Schrade. He then
took 3 or 4 more steps forward and saw Senator Kennedy
lying on the floor with Juan Romero
holding his head.

"Eppridge stopped and took pictures of Senator Kennedy.
Forward was a mass of people around the individual
who apparently shot Senator Kennedy.

"Eppridge did not go forward to see this individual
and stayed in the area of Senator Kennedy."[158]

Cameraman Jim Wilson Recalls

Jim Wilson, John Lewis and Bob Funk
were part of a team filming RFK
in Oregon and California.

Wilson prior to RFK's victory speech
had met with RFK and Bill Barry
in RFK's suite
to "discuss coverage of the speech."

261

Wilson asked RFK for permission to "let him
precede them into the Embassy Room
for filming purposes."

Permission was granted and Wilson, Lewis and Funk
hastened downstairs five flights
in time to film RFK and party
enter the room and up upon the stage.

Wilson stood on a chair on the stage
and filmed the speech
including to the point where
RFK reached the rear curtain of the stage.

He followed RFK and party down the corridor
toward the swinging doors
leading to the pantry.

Shooting began
The film crew was about 15 rows of people
away from the Senator

He spotted RFK on the floor
and "moved forward filming to within five
feet of the Senator and dropped to his knees.

Wilson used about three minutes of film left in his camera,
then stopped filming
and started helping clear away oglers
from around RFK

too upset to continue filming.[159]

Toward the Ice Machine

With more than ten minutes
advance knowledge
he'd leave
on the route of ice,

They stationed Sirhan there,
in the pantry by the ice machine

with his handler or sitter
        the woman in the polka-dot dress

(and the actual hitman too
        in place in place in place).

She was whispering his
        final wire-up

Maybe a code phrase
        such as that given to Candy Jones
                to place her in action.

On the right was a large
        floor-to-ceiling ice-making machine.
At the end of the ice machine
        situated in an indentation, was a low tray stacker
        upon which (or next to which)
                Sirhan and the woman
                had stood.

(see photo of tray stacker later in this poem).

On the left were two stainless steel steam tables
        that narrowed the passage
        at one spot to about 6 feet.

There was a young woman named Lisa Urso,
a high school student in San Diego
who was standing by the door of the pantry

as RFK entered the pantry.

Suddenly she was shoved from behind
and a young man pushed in front of her.
"I thought it was going to be a waiter
and it looked like he was trying to get
                in there
        & shake the Senator's hand."

It was Sirhan Sirhan. She saw a flash from the gun.

Lisa Urso also spotted another person,
a blond wearing a gray suit with a gun in his hand.
It was not Sirhan, and not wearing a uniform.[160]

RFK researcher Philip Melanson interviewed another witness—
whom he listed under a pseudonym Martha Raines to protect her—
who saw a guy with dark wavy hair in a gray suit shoot his gun
(once or twice) and run out of the pantry. He was seen with
Sirhan earlier in the evening.[161]

As I said, Sirhan had been spotted by an Ambassador waiter
standing on a metal table with
a woman wearing a polka-dot dress.

Polka-dot and Sirhan were talking
then Sirhan dismounted the table.
(see below, Sirhan's memory of
Polka-dot sitting on the table.)

Yet, as He Fired at RFK, Sirhan Thought He Was Shooting at Circle Targets at a Firing Range

From Dr. Daniel Brown's hypnosis sessions with Sirhan:

"Mr. Sirhan was led to the kitchen
by a woman after that same woman
had received directions from an official of the event.
Mr. Sirhan did not go with the intent to shoot Senator Kennedy,
but did respond to a specific hypnotic cue given to him
by that woman to enter 'range mode,' during which
Mr. Sirhan automatically and involuntarily responded with
a 'flashback' that he was shooting
at circle targets . . . (and)
did not know . . . that he was shooting at Senator Kennedy."[162]

—page 8, Exhibit I, Declaration of Dr. Daniel Brown

Sirhan to Dr. Brown (when he and Polka-dot
arrive in the kitchen): "I'm still sleepy . . . very sleepy . . .
I was flirting with her . . . the place was darkish . . .
we were the only ones in that area . . . I don't know
where the hell it was . . . a deep place to get romantic with

264

"Look, look, look."

that girl . . . Then she sat up on the table facing with her back
to the wall . . . her thighs and legs are right here . . .
I am just looking at her trying to take
her beauty in . . . I am trying to figure out how to hit on her. . . .
That's all I can think about . . . She sat on the steam table.
I was leaning. I was fascinated with her looks . . . She was
sitting. I was standing. I was engrossed. She was busty,
looked like Natalie Wood. She never said much. It
was very erotic. I was consumed by her. She was
a seductress with an unspoken availability."

Sirhan to Dr. Brown: "I'm trying to figure out
how I'm going to have her . . . All of a sudden she's looking
over my head toward an area . . .
Then she taps or pinches me . . . It is startling . . ."

Dr. Brown then asked Sirhan what exactly he remembers
after she tapped or pinched him.

Sirhan: "It was like a wake-up . . . the contact with my body . . .
This is too abnormal for people to pinch like that for
no given reason. It was like when you're stuck with a pin
or pinched . . . a very sharp pinch . . . I thought she did it
with her fingernails . . . like a wake-up . . . it snapped me
out of my doldrums . . . yet I'm still sleepy . . .

"She points back over my head . . . .
She says, 'Look, look, look.' I turn around. . . .
I don't know what happened after that . . .

"She spun me around or turned my body around . . .
She was directing my attention to the rear . . . Way back . . .
There are people coming back through the doors . . .
I am still puzzled about what she is directing me to . . .
It didn't seem relevant to me . . . Some people started
streaming in . . . She kept motioning toward the back . . .
Then all of a sudden she gets more animated . . .
She put her arm on my shoulder . . .

"I think she had her hand on me . . . I am not sure if it
was her hand or somebody else's. Then I
was at the target range . . . a flashback to the target range . . .
I thought that I was at the range more than I was
actually shooting at any person . . ."[163]

—pages 11–12 Exhibit I, Declaration of Dr. Daniel
Brown, 2011

Dr. Brown:
Sirhan Sirhan "thought he was firing
at stationary circle targets
at a firing range. He did
not know he was firing
at Senator Kennedy
at the time of
the assassination."

"On the night of the assassination, all
that was required was for (Sirhan Sirhan) to
show up at a designated place induced
by post-hypnotic suggestion, be led to
the site by a handler, and then adopt
'range mode' upon cue."[164]

The Actual Shooter May Have Shoved Waiter
DiPierro Aside to Get Close to RFK

As RFK left the stage, turned to his right, and walked down
an incline and through the double swinging doors that led
to the kitchen serving area,
there were four key persons very near him—Karl Uecker
(Ambassador maître d'), Edward Minasian (of the Ambassador
catering department), waiter Vincent DiPierro, and waiter
Martin Patrusky.

Added to these four is possibly the man who shot RFK at very
close range
into his brain through his right mastoid.

Key to understanding RFK's final few seconds
are the statements of Ambassador waiter
Vincent DiPierro to the FBI.
DiPierro was not working on June 4, but went to the
Ambassador to witness the celebration of RFK's victory.

He arrived not long before RFK's speech.
DiPierro went to the kitchen and pantry area.
As he told the FBI, "My reason for doing this

267

was to shake hands with Senator Kennedy.
Shortly after this Senator Kennedy entered this room
and then exited to the Embassy Room [to give his speech].
As he went out the door to the Embassy Room Senator Kennedy
shook hands with me. . . .

"I remained by the door leading to the Embassy Room
and shortly thereafter, Eddie Minasian, another hotel employee,
told me that Senator Kennedy was finishing his speech
and that he was going to the Colonial Room for a press conference
and that I was to make an aisle for him.
Senator Kennedy, after his speech, then left the stage
in the Embassy Room and went through a door at the rear
of the stage. He then turned to his right,
walked down a ramp and was then in the same room
as I was. As Senator Kennedy walked through this room
I began walking next (approx. 3 feet) to him.

"Senator Kennedy walked through the swinging door
on the left side and I went through the swinging door
on the right side. At this time we were both
(Senator Kennedy and I) in the kitchen."

Shooter Possibly Suddenly Walking Next to Kennedy

DiPierro continued: "There were approx. 40-50 people
in this pantry room including hotel employees and spectators.
I was walking next to Senator Kennedy while in the pantry area
and at that time another unknown individual
walked between myself and Senator Kennedy.
At that time I was then walking approx. 5 feet away
and slightly behind Senator Kennedy."

The FBI reported "DiPierro stated that he first
saw Sirhan Bishara Sirhan approximately one minute
before the shooting standing on a tray holder
six inches high
located approximately 30 feet from where he (DiPierro)
was standing."

(DiPierro said Sirhan was standing next to a girl
with a "pudgy nose" wearing a "white dress with black
or purple polka dots on it.)

"DiPierro stated that Sirhan
was holding on to the tray holder
          with his left hand
and his right hand
          was across his body."

and "DiPierro stated that when he saw
Sirhan Bishara Sirhan
          standing next to the girl,
She was leaning over Sirhan
standing next to her
          and Sirhan
                    was smiling
                         at her."[165]

Police Photo of Assassination Scene in Kitchen, Tray Stacker on Left on which Sirhan Stood Talking with Polka-Dot, then Sirhan Dismounted as RFK Entered the Room

"As Senator Kennedy shook the hand of the hotel cook
he then turned to his right in the direction of the heating cabinet
and at that time I saw the white male who was previously standing
on the tray holder now standing behind Mr. Uecker

269

at the heating cabinet. I saw this individual reach his right arm
around Mr. Uecker and in his hand he had a revolver
which was pointed directly at Senator Kennedy's head.
The revolver was about 3–5 feet from Senator Kennedy's head.
This individual then shot Senator Kennedy in the head.
Senator Kennedy at this time threw his hands and arms up,
reeled backwards and fell to the floor. During this period of time
and after the first shot was fired I heard 3 more rapidly fired shots. . . .

"The same white male that I saw standing on the tray holder
is the same person who stood behind Mr. Uecker and shot
Senator Kennedy and was later taken away by Los Angeles Police
officers after being captured by Mr. Johnson, Mr. Grier and Mr. Uecker. . . .
(signed) Vincent DiPierro."

Vincent DiPierro also told the FBI "that the white female
standing on the tray holder with the gunman would be described as
follows:

> White, female, 5'4"-5'6", 21 to 25 years of age,
> dark brown hair, shapely figure wearing a white dress,
> described as form fitting, with a scoop neck and ruffled collar,
> and the dress appeared to have black or dark violet
> polka dots.

> "He stated that he thought he might recognize her again
> if he saw her, but did not have the opportunity to observe
> her after the shooting occurred."

Rafer Johnson Recalls the Evening, Going in the Elevator to the Embassy Ballroom, the Speech, Getting Separated from RFK, the Shooting, the Aftermath

Rafer Johnson arrived at the Ambassador at 8 p.m. on June 4.
Around 8:30 he went to the RFK suite of rooms on the 5th floor.
He checked in with Bill Barry, then waited in the suite, talking
with Ethel and other friends.

At approximately 11 p.m. RFK went to the fourth floor
                              for an interview on tv
Then returned to the fifth floor "and was interviewed

in a television studio which was set up on that
floor. Johnson accompanied Kennedy during the interview."

Around midnight or not long thereafter
the party in the suite "began to leave the suite."

RFK was accompanied by Rafer Johnson and Bill Barry.
They went down to the ground floor on the freight elevator.

> "When the elevator stopped and the doors opened
> Johnson observed that they were in the kitchen or
> serving area of the hotel and he presumed that it was the
> same floor where Senator Kennedy was to make his speech.

> "Barry was leading Senator Kennedy. Johnson
> was following behind the Senator and Roosevelt Grier
> with Mrs. Kennedy behind him. After leaving the
> elevator Senator Kennedy stopped when a man dressed
> in a white uniform, presumably a kitchen worker,
> reached across the table to shake his hand.

> "Johnson moved toward this individual and raised
> his arm to keep him away. Senator Kennedy reached
> across Johnson's arm and shook hands with this man.
> The Senator then moved ahead five feet and greeted another
> male kitchen worker. The Senator may have also
> shaken hands with a fourth kitchen employee . . . "

> "Rafer Johnson and Mr. and Mrs. George Plimpton became
> separated from the Senator because some member of a CBS
> camera crew was pulling a cable in the corridor
> and blocked their passage for a few moments."

Rafer then went up onto the stage, from steps to the right
if you face the stage. "During this time Barry and Johnson
were standing together and he questioned Barry as to how
the Senator planned to leave the stage upon the conclusion
of the speech. Barry indicated that the exit would be made
the same way as they previously entered the stage.

"Shortly before the end of Kennedy's speech, Barry
moved toward the Senator. Senator Kennedy turned from the
podium and started towards the side of the stage by which

he had previously entered. Senator Kennedy paused
for a moment and then turned to the opposite
direction (left side of stage). Johnson could not see
whether the Senator continued to the far left of the stage,
but did notice that his direction of travel was slightly towards
the rear.

"Johnson realized that the Senator was leaving the stage
by a different way and attempted to reach him but because
of the crowd he could not move forward. Johnson, in the
company of Mrs. Plimpton, walked to the back of the stage
(right side) near the corridor and joined Senator Kennedy
as he walked past. . . .

"As Senator Kennedy walked past Johnson, he noticed that
Barry and unrecalled other individuals were in front of the
Senator. Between Senator Kennedy and Johnson, who
were approximately five feet apart, there was a camera man
and a sound man, identities unknown. Johnson and Mrs.
Plimpton continued to follow Senator Kennedy through
a darkened area and at a point, three or four feet from
an opened double doorway with a divider at the center,
Johnson heard a sound which reminded him of a bursting
balloon. A second or two later, Johnson heard a second similar
sound and looking in the direction where he assumed the
Senator should have been, he saw smoke and fragments
of paper in the air.

"The area in front of Johnson was brightly lit possibly by
camera lights. After hearing the second noise, Johnson
immediately assumed that these noises were gunshots.

"Johnson immediately moved forward pushing people
aside. Due to the great number of people in the area
forward movement was seriously impaired. As he passed
through the open double doors he saw Barry
                    hit and push a white male who
                    was standing on the floor in
                    front of him (Johnson)
                    but slightly to the right.

"Johnson continued to push forward and observed
a wounded man lying on the floor
in front of the doorway.

"He saw blood on this person's forehead and also
thought that he saw a bullet hole in the top of his head.

"Johnson then observed Senator Kennedy lying on the
floor in the same area. The Senator was lying on
his back in an almost flat position but looked as if
he was struggling to get up.

"His left arm was on the floor, his right arm moved from
a down position beside his head through an arch
and down to his side. Johnson saw blood on the floor
beneath the right side of Kennedy's head below the ear
and extending down the right cheek and down the
                    right side of his chest.
Senator Kennedy looked at Johnson and they stared
at each other for a moment."

Johnson told the FBI he then decided whether to help
the Senator or go to Bill Barry to help subdue
                    the guy with the gun.

The guy still had it in hand.
"Johnson lunged at the man and grasped the
                    front part of the gun with his left hand.
Roosevelt Grier had the butt end of the gun in his hand."
Sirhan still had "his finger on the trigger housing."
Grier twisted the weapon from the gunman's hand
and Johnson noticed that Bill Barry now
                    was at the Senator's side.

Those holding Sirhan included Johnson, Grier,
George Plimpton, and two hotel employees

Rafer told Rosey "Rosey, let me have the gun."
He said it twice, then Grier handed him the .22.
Johnson placed it in his left pocket.
He then asked the man, "Why did you do it?"
No answer. "Johnson, moving his face directly
in front of the assailant and looking directly into his
eyes repeated, 'Why did you do it?' The man
did not respond. Johnson then clenched his
fist and placed the back of his fist on the assailant's
forehead. Johnson then repeated, 'Why did you do it?'

The assailant answered, 'I'll explain it.' The assailant did not speak any other words while he was in Johnson's presence."

(Johnson later that night was driven to LAPD headquarters where he turned in the gun. Further he did not recall the polka-dot dress, nor see anyone running from the shooting scene after the shots.)[166]

Jesus Perez, the Final Person to Shake RFK's Hand in the Pantry,

was a kitchen helper who had worked at the Ambassador for 13 years.

He and other workers were standing in the pantry shortly before midnight
                    watching the speech on TV.

Perez told the FBI "that approximately one half hour before midnight, the man who was later identified as Sirhan Sirhan, was also in the pantry of
        the Ambassador Hotel, and appeared to be just
        another curious onlooker waiting to get a glimpse
                    of the celebrities.

    "He stated that Sirhan asked him and the other
    kitchen employees three or four times if they were
    sure that Senator Kennedy would pass that way as he
    left the Embassy Ballroom. Perez advised that he
    simply told Sirhan that he did not know.

    Perez noticed "that he, Sirhan, had some type of
    papers in his hands and that he was folding them
    or twisting them in some way, which gave the
    impression that he was nervous."

    Then about 15–20 minutes after midnight
    RFK and his party entered the pantry.
    Perez told the FBI "that all of the people
    in the pantry, including himself and his fellow workers,
    pressed forward to greet the Senator and attempted
    to shake his hand. Perez stated that he was

shaking the Senator's hand, or rather the Senator
was just letting go of his hand after having
greeted him, when he heard a noise which sounded
like a gun shot or firecracker."

Perez turned his head and saw Sirhan Sirhan "waving
his arm with an object in his hand, which Perez
recognized as a revolver." Perez saw Sirhan
fire "several more shots just as several men grabbed him
in an attempt to subdue him and take away the pistol."[167]

Evan Freed Was There

According to excellent RFK researcher Philip Melanson,
a freelance photographer named Evan Freed
had stepped inside the pantry
                to repair his damaged camera
when there were shots
and he was pushed against the wall
                by the shove of bodies,
                so that Freed fell backward.

Getting back his balance, he saw the struggle to
                disarm Sirhan.

Freed also saw three people—two men and a woman
running to the exit at the east end of the pantry.

One of the men was wearing a light blue sport coat
and, in the words of Melanson, "it seemed to Freed
that this man was being chased by the third man."

As for the woman, Freed told LAPD that the woman
was Caucasian and "possibly wearing a polka-dot dress."[168]

Freed Sees a Second Person
Aiming a Gun

News photographer Evan Freed
Who later was LA deputy city attorney,

had been in the RFK suite on the fifth floor
then accompanied RFK on the elevator
                    down to his triumphal speech.

Prior to the speech's conclusion,
Freed went into the kitchen pantry
"There he noticed two men 'very similar in appearance'
moving around. One of these men would turn out to be
Sirhan. The two men did not stand together,
                    but seemed to look at each other every
                    now and then. . . . "

RFK entered the pantry after his speech
and Evan Freed said he was walking by his side.

He was about "four feet away" when shooting started

Freed: "I saw the second man (wearing darker clothing)
who had been in the pantry with Sirhan during the speech
                    pointing a gun
                    in an upward angle at the Senator.
                    Based on the sound I heard,
                    I believe the first shot
                            came from this man's gun.

        "In the background I could see Sirhan firing
        a revolver held in his right hand
                    in the direction of the Senator.
                    People in the crowd
                            were screaming and grabbing Sirhan. . . ."

Freed further stated in his affidavit
        that people rushed toward Sirhan
        and passed the second gunman
                who was backing away.

Right away Freed viewed the second shooter
        running in his direction
        chased by another man who yelled
                "Stop that guy, stop him!"
Both men, recalled Freed, ran out of the pantry.

(This account is from Evan Freed's 4-page 1992 affidavit.)[169]

Three shots from behind at very, very close range

Frank Burns Sees a Man in a Tuxedo Parting the Curtains at the Stage's Back and Beckoning to RFK

Important RFK supporter, attorney Frank Burns,
arrived at the Ambassador about 7 p.m. on 6-4
and went to the Presidential Suite, the headquarters
for Speaker Unruh and the Kennedy campaign staff.

"Between then and approximately 11:00 p.m.
I was either in the Presidential Suite or around the corner
in the Royal Suite area, which was occupied by
Senator Kennedy and his staff."

Around 11 p.m. Burns went from the 5th floor
down to the Embassy Room to speak
with various people staffing the "anchor desk"
located to the right rear of the speakers podium
About 11:30 "we decided that it was time for
Senator Kennedy to come down, and I went
upstairs to get him. The crowd
was so dense in the Embassy Room
that I went along the passageway
in back of the podium and
through the kitchen, exiting into
the lobby near the front desk."

California Assembly Speaker Jesse Unruh was
just leaving Senator Kennedy's room as Frank Burns
entered. "He told me that they had
decided that Senator Kennedy would
wait a few more minutes before
coming down, but that he, Unruh,
would go down and talk to
the crowd right away."

Mr. Burns escorted Unruh and staff down to the podium.
"While Speaker Unruh was talking, he told me
to get the Senator to come down, and I told
Jack Crose to go upstairs to get him."

Then RFK's brother-in-law, Stephen Smith,
spoke to the crowd.

"As he was concluding Senator Kennedy came into the room
from the door immediately to the left of the podium"

Burns told the FBI that a path had been cleared to the right
"leading toward the area where the anchor desk was located."
RFK then started to move "to his right toward
      the cleared path. I turned to my right
      and at that time I heard a voice coming from my
      left rear saying that the Senator was
      going the wrong way, and that he should
      come off the rear of the platform."

      Burns: "I turned to my left and saw a man in a tuxedo,
      folding the curtains back and beckoning
                    to the Senator to follow him.
      This man stepped down into the anteroom
      and Senator Kennedy followed him.

      "The man went out the door at the back of the
      anteroom, and turned to the right and headed down
      incline with Senator Kennedy close behind him.

      "When I came out of the doorway and turned to the
      right to head down the incline, the man in the
               tuxedo leading Senator Kennedy
               was perhaps 10 feet in front of me
               and moving quite fast.

      "They passed into the kitchen through the left
      hand door which was open. At about that time
      I yelled to slow down because they were
               getting ahead of everyone.

      "My eyes were constantly on the Senator
               as I was trying to attract his attention.

      "As Senator Kennedy approached the area of the
      serving tables, two people moved toward him.
      The one nearest the serving table was very short
and the other one was about medium height.
They both appeared to be dressed in white
kitchen jackets. The Senator stopped and turned
to his left to shake hands with them.

"I would judge that he turned slightly
more than 90° from his original
direction of travel.

"It was when he stopped to shake hands that I caught
up with him and got perhaps a half step in front of him.
I also turned to my left and was facing the same
direction as the Senator. It was at this moment that
I heard a noise
sounding something like a string of firecrackers going off.

"I immediately turned my head to the right.
I have an impression of people standing there,
but I would not be able to positively identify anyone.
The one clear impression I have is of an extended arm
holding a gun.

"This arm appeared to be next to the serving table
and the gun would be about even with the front edge
of the serving table. The arm did not appear to me
to belong to anyone.

"I immediately glanced to my left toward the Senator
and he was falling backward. He had thrown
his hands up and his body appeared to
be spinning to the left.

"I looked back toward the gun, and by then the
person holding the gun had stepped forward
past the edge of the serving table so that he was
directly in front of me. He was aiming the gun
down toward Senator Kennedy's falling body,
and appeared to be shooting at him. My
impression is that the noise of the gunfire had
ceased by then.

"This is the first time I recall seeing the person
later identified as Sirhan Sirhan. At that time
somebody grabbed Sirhan from behind.
Someone else appeared to grab his gun arm
and I grabbed him from the side.

**Confusing situation at the close of the victory speech.
Kennedy acts to move off-stage by side stairs but is
interrupted by a voice of a man pulling aside the
curtain to the back, "This way, Senator."**

"The struggle then became very confused
and we rotated around several times, moving
down the line of the serving counter
in the direction that Senator Kennedy
had originally been traveling.

"The entire situation was chaotic, and I have
only vague impressions of the people who were
wrestling with the assassin at that time. The next
thing I remember clearly is Bill Barry coming up
and plunging into the knot of people, yelling
for a rope so that we could tie him up.

"I remember taking off my belt and handing it
to Barry and bending down to grab the assassin's
legs as to get him off his feet. I believe that Barry
then left and after further struggle, the assassin
      was more or less wrestled onto the top
      of the serving tables."

Burns saw RFK on his back. He told the FBI,
"Everyone was screaming and yelling for a doctor."

Burns then jumped on the serving table
to see where the gun was. He noticed
the gun was in Rosey Grier's hand.

"I then jumped off the table and went around
to the other side because it appeared that the
people that had Sirhan's head
      were trying to pull it off.
He was on his back with his head and upper back
off the edge of the table, and I was afraid they
would push down and break his back.

"The only other person that I remember clearly
is someone in a tuxedo with blond hair,
who had ahold of the assassin's head."

Burns later led police officers
with the handcuffed Sirhan out
      to a waiting squad car.[170]

Witnesses Seeing Sirhan and Polka-Dot

1. George Green, real estate salesman; 2. Jack Merritt, Ace Security guard; 3. Richard Houston, RFK supporter; 4. Darnell Johnson, RFK campaign worker; 5. Dr. Marcus McBroom; 6. Jeanette Prudhomme, RFK volunteer; and seven others "who had noticed the woman in a polka-dot dress earlier in the evening."

Here's uniformed Ace Security guard Jack Merritt's memory, as reported both to the FBI and the LAPD:

> He saw "two men and a woman
> leaving the kitchen." He
> described the woman as about 5 feet five inches tall, having
> "light colored hair."
> The men departing the kitchen
> wore suits, and the woman
> a polka-dot dress.
>
> "They seemed to be smiling,"
> said Mr. Merritt.[171]

FBI Interviews George Green on June 7, 1968. Green Notices Polka-Dot and a Man Running Away after Shooting

> George Green, part of the Kennedy campaign,
> told the FBI that he was coming through the kitchen area doorway
> just as the shots were being fired.
>
> "Green stated that once inside the kitchen door,
> he noticed a woman in her 20s with long blond
> free flowing hair in a polka-dot dress and a light colored
> sweater and a man 5'11", thin build, black hair
> and in his 20's.
>
> "Green stated that this man and woman were running
> with their backs toward him and
> they were attempting to get out of the kitchen area.
> Green stated that the reason he noticed them
> was that they were the only ones who seemed

to be trying to get out of the kitchen area
while everyone else seemed to be trying
                    to get into the kitchen

"Green stated that he then jumped up on top of a food
preparation table to try to assist Rafer Johnson and Roosevelt Grier
who were subduing the male who had a gun in his hand."[172]

George Green Interviewed by FBI Again on 7-16-68

George Green arrived at the Ambassador around 10:30–10:45.

He went to the press room (the Colonial Room).
"He went through the kitchen passageway to the rear
of the press room." At approximately 11:15–11:30 "he noticed
Sirhan Sirhan at the edge of the crowd near a tall thin
person and a female caucasian. Sirhan Sirhan
was wearing blue jeans, a shirt, a jacket and desert boots. . . .
The tall thin person standing near him was approximately
22 years. . . . (Green didn't recall his dress nor ethnic type)

"The female caucasian was in her early twenties
and she wore a polka dot dress which was white
                    with black polka dots.

"She had a good figure, but he cannot further describe her. . . ."[173]

Darnell Johnson and Polka-Dot

Just after RFK finished his speech and walked
                    to the back of the speech platform,
Darnell Johnson walked around the platform
                    & along to the serving area where the shooting
                    would occur.

Johnson got there before RFK and observed five humans
                    already in the area. In the words of the FBI report:

"(1) White female wearing a white dress, with 25¢ size black
polkadots; the dress was fitted, was not miniskirt but was above
the knees; was not a loose shift but was fashionable for the time.

284

She was 23-25 years of age, tall, 5'8", medium build, well built, 145 pounds, long light brown hair, carrying an all white sweater or jacket, pretty full face, stubby heels shoes in the fashion of the time.

"(2) A person whom Johnson identified as Sirhan Sirhan from photographs shown at the time of this interview and further as the person he saw who was seized immediately following the shooting by persons in the area.

"(3) A white male, wearing a light blue washable sport coat, white shirt and tie, 6'1", tall, slim, 30-35 years, blond hair parted far over on the left side with the right side long and hanging toward his face like a surfer haircut, outdoor type.

"(4) A white male, 5'10" tall, 165 pounds, trim, 24–25 years of age, brown, long hair but not hippie, dark coat, darker trousers, white shirt and tie.

"(5) A white male, 6'1", tall slim, darkish-brown hair, shiny brown sport coat made of hopsacking, white shirt and tie."

These five were standing in a group between Johnson and the door through which RFK came into the serving area. He said he had no knowledge they knew one another, or talked together.

"As the Kennedy party entered this area, balloons were being broken, some small firecrackers were being set off and Johnson was not aware of
any difficulties or any trouble until
he saw a woman slump against the wall
and say, 'Oh my God, Oh my God.'

"Johnson still did not realize what had happened
but saw a furor around the Kennedy party.

"At this time a photographer with lights on his camera
took a picture of someone on the floor, who turned out
to be Kennedy. . . ."

The photographer said, "Grab him, that dude has a gun."

FBI: "Just at this point, the woman in the polka dot dress
and the three men in her area left and walked toward
the ballroom from where the Kennedy party had just come."

The crowd began pummeling Sirhan.

"While Sirhan was being held and before police arrived,
the girl in the polka dot dress and the one man in the
light blue washable sport coat came back
        and looked, then both left again."[174]

Dr. McBroom Spots a Calm Polka-Dot Moving toward the Exit

Kennedy supporter Dr. Marcus McBroom, PhD,
was at the Ambassador, arriving about 10:30.

He entered the Embassy Room via the kitchen
The FBI report on an interview with McBroom, dated 7-11-68,
states: "While he was going through the kitchen . . . he observed Sirhan
        sitting on a table in the kitchen."

McBroom joined the celebration in the Embassy Room
        & was invited by Jean Smith to join the "private after-party"
        (apparently meaning at the discotheque, The Factory).

After the speech, McBroom followed RFK and supporters through the
        swinging door into the pantry

        "Just as he entered the door, he heard what he assumed
        later to be the first of several gun shots fired. . . ."

Then he saw Roosevelt Grier and others
        trying to dislodge the .22 from Sirhan's hand.

McBroom then raced thence to try to locate a doctor.
        "While running into the Embassy Room, he stated
he remembers seeing a caucasian female about twenty-five,
5'4", 126 pounds, moving toward the exit. This
woman was wearing a white dress with black polka dots. . . .
The only unusual thing he noticed about this woman was
the fact that she appeared much calmer than anyone else
                in the room,
                and appeared to be trying to leave
                the room as soon as possible."

As McBroom raced from the pantry to locate a doctor,
he saw another man hastening away from the scene
in a furtive way.[175]

Dr. Marcus McBroom Also Spots
Man with Gun under a Newspaper
Leaving the Kitchen

Researcher Greg Stone (in 1986) interviewed McBroom:
"The first inference that we had that anything was awry
was that we heard the first one or two shots. And then a woman
in a polka dot dress ran out of the kitchen shouting 'We got him'
or 'We shot him.' No one really was even certain as to what
she had said because no one initially really comprehended what
was really happening. Immediately after she ran out, a man
with a gun under a newspaper ran out in a very menacing way and
myself and a man by the name of Sam Strain and the man running
the ABC camera, we drew back immediately when we saw the gun."[176]

> Sirhan the patsy
> The man in the suit doing the actual hit
> probably immediately while Sirhan
> was firing, the hitman placing his gun
> very, very near the back of RFK's head,
>   according to the official autopsy
>   no more than two or three inches away—

> a head shot.

> (And Sirhan was never
>   according to a group of witnesses
>   who testified at the Grand Jury,
>   closer than around 3–6 feet from RFK.)

(Some researchers think they've located
the actual RFK shooter,
          who reportedly owns & lives in a
          house, age 75
          in Berkeley, in recent years.)

Lisa Urso

The young woman named Lisa Urso
    as we have noted,
a high school student in San Diego,
was standing by the door of the pantry

as RFK entered the pantry.

Suddenly she was shoved from behind
and a young man pushed in front of her.
"I thought it was going to be a waiter
and it looked like he was trying to get
              in there
      & shake the Senator's hand."

It was Sirhan Sirhan. She saw a flash from the gun.

Urso's view of Kennedy and Sirhan, she claimed, was unobstructed.

"According to Urso, the Senator was walking forward but turned
his head leftward toward a busboy who wanted to shake hands.
When he was shot, Kennedy had not completely turned to face
the busboy but was still facing slightly forward, about to shake hands.

"Urso remains puzzled by the double-motion reaction she claims
to have observed: Kennedy grabbed his head behind the right ear
and jerked forward about six inches before moving in the opposite
direction and falling backward. Why this motion, she wonders, if
Sirhan fired from the direction the Senator first moved toward. . . ."[177]

The Second Gunman Was Seen by Three Witnesses

1. Lisa Urso also spotted another person,
a blond wearing a gray suit with a gun in his hand.
It was not Sirhan, and not wearing a uniform.[178]

2. As we have previously reported,
RFK researcher Philip Melanson interviewed another witness
whom he listed under a pseudonym Martha Raines to protect her—
who saw a guy with dark wavy hair in a gray suit shoot his gun

(once or twice) and run out of the pantry. This man was seen with Sirhan earlier in the evening.[179]

&3. As we have previously noted, photographer Evan Freed recalled that he had walked with RFK through the pantry doors and had seen Sirhan firing
but also
"I saw the second man (wearing darker clothing)
who had been in the pantry with Sirhan
during the speech
pointing a gun
at an upward angle at the Senator.
Based on the sound I heard
I believe the first shot
came from this man's gun."[180]

Sirhan had also been spotted
by an Ambassador waiter
standing on a metal table with
a woman wearing a polka-dot dress.

Polka-dot and Sirhan were talking,
then Sirhan dismounted the table.

Coroner Thomas Noguchi's Account of the Three Bullets in RFK from the Back

1. bullet thru
Kennedy's armpit

2. another bullet lodged in
RFK's spinal column

3. the 3rd bullet, which
killed him
penetrated RFK's skull
just to the left of
his right ear
& subsequently shattered.

Based on Noguchi's analysis of
powder burns behind RFK's ear, he was shot

just an inch from
Kennedy's right ear-edge

Bullets Fired in an Upward Path

According to Thomas Noguchi's meticulous autopsy,
all three bullets that struck RFK
were fired to his back
at an upward angle
(as if the shooter were crouched down—
perhaps to avoid the bullets of Sirhan
fired from the front).

Kennedy Supporter Nina Rhodes-Hughes Recalls Shots at RFK as Coming from Two Directions

Nina Rhodes-Hughes was a campaign fundraiser
and worked on a wine and cheese gathering for Ethel.

June 4 she was celebrating at the Ambassador.
She was on the stage behind the Senator
& followed him, post-speech, toward the kitchen.

She was six to seven feet behind him and to RFK's left.
"He turns to his left a little bit and starts
to greet some of the kitchen staff.

"Then," she recalled, "as I'm looking at him, I heard
'pop pop.'"

She saw several RFK bodyguards grab Sirhan
after two shots were fired.

Then, though Sirhan was held to her left,
more shots rang out to her right,
very near behind RFK.

"The shots," she recalled, are pop, pop, pop, pop, pop. . . ."
They were very rapid, maybe 12–13 in total.

Coroner to the stars

The first two shots from Sirhan to her right
Then more shots, from her right.

Then she collapsed and fainted, coming to
to see Ethel crouched near her husband.

(Nina Rhodes-Hughes was shocked for the
first time, decades later, to read an FBI report
stating that she heard only 8 shots,
          when it was a good number more she heard).[181]

Cues for Post-Hypnotic Suggestions, Say, to Kill

Researcher/writer Martin Lee,
with whom I worked in 1978–'79 on research
          into hypno-robo issues,
located an article in the *Journal of Personal &*
                              Social Psychology,
          Vol. 9, #2, 1968,
(by Martin Orne, Peter Sheehan, & Fred J. Evans
of the University of Penn Hospital & University of Penn),

that stated that once the post-hypnotic cue
          (to trigger a specific act)
          is established deeply, then any person
          who gives the cue
                    can evoke programmed responses.

Thus, even though Sirhan Sirhan had been programmed,
say, by the man with the pencil mustache,

Polka-dot could have delivered the
                    cue to shoot.[182]

The Record Is Clear on Polka-Dot Dress

So, the historical record is clear
that there was a woman in a polka-dot dress
who ran from one of the doors of the Embassy Ballroom
leading to the outside,
          shouting something like, "We shot him! We killed him!"

(You can read more in William Turner's and Jonn Christian's *The Assassination of Robert F. Kennedy.* Try around page 67.)

As far back as two years after June '68 it was written, "It turns out that six . . . witnesses saw the girl in the polka dot dress with Sirhan before the shots and afterward."

(Sandy Serrano and Vincent DiPierro, plus four more and those listed by Philip Melanson)[183]

Polka-Dot Herself Programmed?

> Was Polka-dot herself
> programmed
>   to deliver
>   a preset signal
>   for Sirhan
>   to shoot?

Here's the Text from Dr. Brown's Report That Sirhan Thought He Was Shooting at Targets at a Gun Range

"Sirhan has recalled to Harvard's Dr. Brown that when he fired his .22 in the pantry of the Ambassador Hotel kitchen he believed he was at a gun range and shooting at circular targets. Dr. Brown's statement, contained in an exhibit in a 2011 court case seeking a retrial of Sirhan Sirhan, stated: "Mr. Sirhan did not know and could not have known that Senator Kennedy was going to pass through the kitchen area. Mr. Sirhan was led to the kitchen area by a woman after that same woman had received directions from an official at the event.

"Mr. Sirhan did not go with the intent to shoot Senator Kennedy, but did respond to a specific hypnotic cue given to him by that woman to enter 'range mode,' during which Mr. Sirhan automatically and involuntarily responded with a 'flashback' that he was shooting at a firing range at circle targets. At the time Mr. Sirhan did not know that he was shooting at people nor did he know that he was shooting at Senator Kennedy.

Dr. Brown states how Sirhan recalled
how suddenly polka-dot was looking over his head
"toward an area..." Then she startlingly pinches or taps
him "like when you're stuck with a pin or pinched"
He thought she dug in with her fingernails.
It snapped Sirhan out of his sleepiness.
She spun him around, he recalled, and directed
his attention toward the rear.
She said "Look, look, look"
        and placed her hand on his shoulder.

"Then I was at the target range . . .
a flash back to the shooting range . . . I didn't know that I had a gun . . .
there was this target like a flashback to the target range . . .
I thought that I was at the range more than I was actually shooting
at any person, let alone Bobby Kennedy."

Brown then asked Sirhan to recall his state of mind. "My mental state
was like I was drunk and sleepy . . . maybe the girl had something
to do with it . . . I was like at the range again . . ."

What did the targets look like? Dr. Brown asked. "Circles. Circles . . .
It was like I was at the range again ... I think I shot one or two shots . . .
Then I snapped out of it and thought 'I'm not at the range'
. . .Then, 'What is going on?' Then they started grabbing me . . .
I'm thinking, 'the range, the range, the range.'

"Then everything gets blurry . . . after that first or second shot
. . . that was the end of it . . . It was the wrong place for the gun
to be there . . . I thought it was the range . . . they broke my finger . . ."

Then Sirhan was asked, What happens next? Sirhan: "Next thing
I remember I was being choked and man-handled,
    I didn't know what was going on. I didn't
      realize until they got me in a car . . .
    later when I saw the female judge I knew
that Bobby Kennedy was shot and I was the shooter,
      but it doesn't come into my memory."[184]

Reporter Jules Witcover

The writer Jules Witcover covered the Kennedy campaign
(and later wrote a book on it, *85 Days: The Last Campaign
of Robert Kennedy*).

Kennedy was only about 30 feet
from his destination—the Colonial Room
                    to talk with the press.

"Members of the kitchen staff lined his path
to see him or shake his hand."

Witcover wrote that Karl Uecker was guiding the Candidate
He does not mention security guard Thane Cesar.

At 12:13 a.m. a Mutual radio reporter named Andy West
tape recorder running
                    asked Kennedy how he could overcome
                    Humphrey's delegate count.
Kennedy started to answer, "It just goes back to
                    the struggle for it. . . ."

Witcover: "Then suddenly the young man
stepped down from the tray-stacker, raised his right hand
                    high over
                    the surrounding aides

and fired a snub-nosed revolver at Kennedy's head
at close range,
          probably not more than a few feet."[185]

          78 people
          were in the pantry
          when RFK
                    came through the door.[186]

The Ice Machine Room

One account stated there was a sign,
          THE ONCE AND FUTURE KING
                    taped to the wall

near where Kennedy stopped by the ice machine
to greet those lined and clustered there.

The guard named Thane Eugene Cesar,
          who was helping lead the Candidate toward the kitchen,

had worked a full day at Lockheed
        as a maintenance plumber,
then went home (to Simi) where he received a call
from Ace Guard Service
        (where he worked part-time)
to go to the Ambassador for guard duty that night.
Cesar was assigned to escort Kennedy
        into the Colonial Room.

Maybe Pushing Back the Kitchen Crowd

Mr. Cesar apparently grabbed RFK's right arm
with his left
        and began pushing back the crowd
                in the pantry with his right
before Sirhan fired.

"I was there holding his arm when they shot him,"
        Cesar told a reporter (who was taping)
        minutes after the shooting.

Cesar saw the gun
        and saw a red flash from the muzzle.

The kitchen was not well lit, it is said.
The television lights were off.

However, the security guard Mr. Cesar,
who was conducting RFK from the back of the stage
toward the kitchen, said, according to writer Robert Blair Kaiser,
"'I saw a hand sticking out of the crowd,
between two cameramen, and the hand was holding a gun.' Cesar says
he was blinded by the brilliant lights, moved toward the gun, then saw
a red flash come from the muzzle. 'I ducked,' says Cesar, 'because
I was as close as

Kennedy was. When I ducked, I threw myself off balance and fell back. . . .
And when I hit . . . I fell against the iceboxes and the
        Senator fell down right in front of me."[187]

        (But, were there NO brilliant lights? Or had they
        just been turned off as RFK entered the pantry?)

Thane Eugene Cesar

Cesar later admitted that he drew his gun,
a source of much speculation
                    by conspiracy buffs.

He said he pulled his gun out
                    after the shots
                              and went to Kennedy's side
                                        "to protect him from further attack."

Three Drawn Weapons: Sirhan's, Cesar's, and a Tall Man in a Suit

In the words of excellent researcher Philip Melanson:
"In addition to Sirhan's gun and that of security guard Cesar,
Lisa Urso saw another one. During our interview she clearly recalled
someone she assumed to be a "security guard" drawing a gun.
But Urso's 'guard' was not wearing a uniform. She sighted the gun
immediately after the shooting, just as Sirhan's gun was wrestled
from him.

"'But the security guard had a gun, and I think he went like this
(drawing a gun) or he put it in a holster for something. . . . Somebody
(the 'guard') put it back into a holster.' She described the man as
blond and wearing a gray suit. He was located 'by Kennedy.' Urso
said she had mentioned this 'guard' to the authorities on a couple
of occasions. They reacted with disinterest on one occasion;
hostility, on another.

"A second witness, whom we shall call Martha Raines, told the author
of seeing a man fire a gun in the pantry. He was approximately
6-feet 2-inches tall, Caucasian, with dark, wavy hair and wearing
a suit (not a uniform). Raines had seen the man standing near
Sirhan earlier in the evening. She believed that the man constituted
a sinister presence in the pantry and was not protecting the Senator.

"According to Raines, the man fired a handgun of some kind. She
recalled that the gunman 'was not composed.' He didn't shoot
'more than once or twice' before running out of the pantry.

"'And I recall,' said Raines, 'one of them (the shots) was high
and should have gone into the ceiling. I don't know what those
people found when they did their ballistic tests . . . but it appeared
to me there should have been a gunshot in the ceiling.'"[188]

298

Thane Eugene Cesar's Account to the FBI

Cesar was interviewed on June 11, 1968
"at his place of employment."

Cesar was employed "on a part-time basis"
by the Ace Guard Service, 8720 Woodley Avenue, Sepulveda,
California." He was assigned to the Ambassador the evening of
6-4-68.

He arrived for work at 6:05 and was assigned to the Embassy
     Room for most of the evening.
          "Cesar stated his main function during the early
          part of the evening was to patrol the entrance
          to the Embassy Room, control drunks, break up fights,
          and to keep young children from sneaking into the
          Embassy Room."

Around 10:30 the Embassy Room waxed very crowded
so that "Cesar, at the request of the Los Angeles Fire
Department, was assigned to the kitchen area behind the
Embassy Room."

"Cesar stated his function at that point was
to restrict people from entering the Embassy Room
from the kitchen, allowing admittance only to Kennedy
staff members and members of the working press.

          "At 11:50 p.m., Cesar was moved to the
          exit door leading from the Embassy Room
          to the kitchen area by Fred Murphy,
          Security Guard, Ambassador Hotel.

          "Cesar stated at this time he was informed
          by Murphy the plan was for Senator Kennedy
          to leave the Embassy Room through this door
          after making his victory speech and proceed

                    "through the kitchen to the Colonial Room
                    where a press conference was scheduled
                    to be held.

"At approximately 12:10 a.m.,
Senator Kennedy emerged from the Embassy Room
into the corridor leading to the kitchen

"and Cesar, holding Senator Kennedy's right arm
and holding the crowd back with his right hand,
began to escort the Senator through the crowd.

"As the Senator entered the kitchen from
the corridor, approximately ten feet from
                              a steam table,
Kennedy pulled loose from Cesar's grasp
and proceeded over to shake hands
                              with a busboy.

"At this time, Cesar attempted to stay as close
to Kennedy as possible and at the same time,
trying to control the crowd.

"As Kennedy was shaking hands with a busboy,
Cesar looked up and suddenly saw a hand
sticking out of the crowd between two camera men
                    and the hand was holding a gun.

"Cesar continued that he was blinded by the
brilliant lights and could not see the face
of the individual holding the gun.

"Just as Cesar started to move to jump on the gun,
he saw the red flash come from the muzzle.

"At the same time, Cesar was shoved by an
unknown individual, and the next thing
he remembered he was on the floor
                    against the ice machine.

"Cesar stated he was approximately four feet
from the gun when it went off
and that Senator Kennedy was approximately
                    two feet from the gun.

(Cesar's clip-on tie fell off, and is seen in photos
on the floor next to the fallen Senator.)

300

Cesar's clip-on fell off.

"Cesar scrambled to his feet, drew his gun,
and moved to the Senator.

"At this time, Cesar stated there were several men
on top of the assassin trying to get the
gun from his grasp. Cesar stated he took a position
next to the Senator's body to protect him
                    from further attack,

"and about three minutes later was given orders
by Ambassador Security Guard Murphy
to get to the Embassy Room doors
and keep the crowd out.

"Cesar took his position at the Embassy Room
door inside the Embassy Room
            and stayed there until approximately
            2 a.m. controlling the crowd."[189]

Pete Hamill Observes Shooting
and Someone Lowering RFK to the Floor

Writer Hamill stood on the stage during RFK's speech
and then "saw Senator Kennedy in the pantry.
Hamill was walking along with George Plimpton
in front of Senator Kennedy and to his (RFK's)
right about ten feet.

". . . As Hamill was walking along and looking back,
he saw Senator Kennedy turn to his left to shake hands
with someone. After Senator Kennedy shook hands
with this individual, he (RFK) turned to continue
            walking straight ahead.

"At this time what Hamill thought were five shots
were fired in very rapid succession. Hamill looked
and saw Sirhan Sirhan who was standing in front of
and to Senator Kennedy's left about seven or eight
feet with his (Sirhan's) arm fully extended
and his face in tremendous concentration
                    shooting a gun at Senator Kennedy.

"Senator Kennedy was falling to the floor
and someone caught Senator Kennedy."[190]

Another Witness Recalls Someone
Lowering RFK to the Floor

RFK researcher Lisa Pease wrote:
"Paul Hope of the *Evening Star* also obtained early comments from Cesar. Hope recorded Cesar's comments as follows:

'I fell back and pulled the Senator with me. He slumped to the floor on his back. I was off balance and fell down and when I looked up about 10 people already had grabbed the assailant.'

"Cesar told the LAPD that he ducked and was knocked down at the first shot,
hardly the same report he gave the press.

"Richard Drew witnessed something similar to Cesar's original version, as he reported in a separate article in the *Evening Star* that same day (6/5/68):

'As I looked up, Sen. Kennedy started to fall back and then was lowered to the floor by his aides.'

"In Drew's LAPD interview, he reduced the plural to the singular, saying 'someone' had lowered Kennedy to the floor. Since Kennedy was shot in the back at a range of one to two inches, anyone lowering him to the floor should have been an immediate suspect."[191]

(Did the actual shooter
sort of lower RFK to the floor?)

"Kennedy, you son of a bitch"
is what TV producer Richard Lubic, among
the 78,
thought he heard Sirhan snarl.

(Though, maybe it was not Sirhan Sirhan's snarl
but the second shooter,
the actual hitman,
or perhaps someone else
—a part of the kill squad)[192]

There were shots
Witnesses gave differing accounts of the number.
There was an initial quick popping sound

then a rapid series
                    pop-pop-pop-pop-pop-pop-pop
                                        pop-pop-pop
                                                pop-pop-pop

        (the total number of pops is a matter of discussion
          but more than the 8 in the Iver-Johnson)

But were there brilliant lights?
Accounts say that the TV and photo lights were off
(or switched off just after RFK's entrance
in the crush at the entrance to the kitchen.

Cesar, or someone, could have fired
in the madness of the crush
his pistol
        right up against
                or an inch or two away from
                        RFK's head by the ear.

(One writer later said he gave Mr. Cesar a polygraph test,
and has said that he passed it.)

According to Los Angeles Coroner Thomas Noguchi,
who did the autopsy on Robert Kennedy,

all three bullets that struck Kennedy entered from the rear,
in a bullet-path from down to up, right to left. "Moreover," he noted,
"powder burns around the entry wound indicated that the fatal bullet
was fired at less than one inch from the head and no more than two or
three inches behind the right ear." (And Sirhan
                was never closer than 2–3 feet to RFK.)

The Pruszynski Tape Showing Extra Shots

A Polish reporter named Stanislaw Pruszynski
was covering the primary victory that night
                        for the *Montreal Gazette*.

He happened to have his tape recorder running
during the shooting.

"Kennedy, you son of a bitch."

He later gave the tape to the California State Archives,
where it resided unexamined for a number of decades.

The recording was finally re-examined and digitally remastered;
and forensic examiners contend that at least 14 shots were fired
in the kitchen pantry
during that burst of pop-pop-pops.[193]

Was Sirhan Firing Blanks?

Sirhan's .22 seemed to spit out little pieces of paper,
like a starter's pistol.

Ballistics expert William Harper, who worked on the RFK case,
told Sirhan Sirhan's legal researcher, Lynn Mangan,
that a source in LAPD had said that Sir Sir
was firing blanks.[194]

"It didn't sound like gun shots to me,
& I've heard a lot of gun shots. It sounded
like a cap pistol or somebody cracking a balloon,"

stated Norbert Schlei,
former assistnt attorney general
under JFK and LBJ.[195]

Karl Uecker, who was leading RFK through
the kitchen, told the FBI, 6-5-68, "I—at the time I
didn't recognize what it was, and I saw some paper flying.
I don't even remember what it was, paper
or white pieces of things."

Rafer Johnson also saw it:
"I looked, and then the second shot, I saw smoke
and saw like something from a—like a—the residue
from a bullet or cap, looked like a cap gun throwing
off residue."[196]

After all, the kill team didn't want Sirhan firing wildly,
hitting the actual killer.

Wounded bystanders

(Later Sirhan told investigator Lynn Mangan
that he had met a young man at the Fish Canyon Firing Range
the afternoon of June 4, and that the young man had
received a gun for his eighteenth birthday.
He was firing blanks and shared those blanks with Sirhan.
Sirhan recalled the boy put his blanks in Sirhan's .22,
and they each fired the blanks in each other's weapon
Mangan: "Then suddenly at 5:00 p.m. . . . the range master,
loudly called out, "Time!" That meant all shooting STOPS when
'Time!' is called out. Sirhan's gun still contained all of the unfired
bullets—but he could not remember if the bullets were the blanks"
        when Sirhan
            departed the Fish Canyon Firing Range)[197]

—Lynn Mangan
"Plain Talk 3"
http://www.sirhansresearcher.com/plaintalk3.htm

Wresting the Gun from Sirhan's Grasp

Bill Barry, RFK's main guard, had rushed to
the pantry. He told the FBI a few hours later:

"I took the gun away from him
            and put the gun on the counter."

Sirhan then somehow re-grabbed the gun
and several on hand
            subdued him and seized the weapon.

"I Can Explain. I Can Explain"

Correspondent John Reguly
was sitting in the Colonial Room press room
talking with Hillary Lamb
            when they heard "popping sounds"
            and went to the "kitchen area"

where Reguly saw RFK on the floor
and Rosey Grier had grabbed ahold of the gun
            and had it pointed to the wall.

"Give him air."

"Grier then took the gun from Sirhan
            and passed it to Rafer Johnson." He also
spotted George Plimpton grab Sirhan.

Reguly heard Sirhan say, "I can explain, I can explain," while
            Grier was twisting Sirhan's leg.[198]

Reporter Richard Harwood's Memory of Angry People Shouting, "Kill Him!"

Harwood, covering the campaign for the *Washington Post*,
heard four or five shots

and saw RFK lying on the floor.

He ran to the press room & telephoned
            the *Washington Post*
            to place a hold on the issue,

then returned where RFK lay.
Harwood told the FBI
            "the suspect was being held on a hotel serving
            tray while a crowd of angry persons
                        were screaming to kill him."

(Harwood said Sirhan was wearing
            blue jacket and blue dungarees.)[199]

Harold Hughes

Governor of Iowa, then running for the US Senate
at the encouragement of Robert Kennedy,

was in the Colonial Room
during RFK's victory speech
            watching the speech on closed circuit tv.

Hughes recounted that Herbert Healey opened the
door "from the Colonial Room to the kitchen
to facilitate Senator Kennedy's entrance in the
                        Colonial Room.

"A few moments after Healy opened the door,
Hughes heard what he thought were two series of shots,
possibly 3 or 4 in each series. . . ."

Hughes and others
        pushed into the kitchen
and saw several wrestling with Sirhan
                who still was holding his gun.

Someone yelled, "Break his arm!"

Jesse Unruh clambered upon a table
and shouted, "Don't kill him.
                        Let him stand trial."

(Additional pages from Hughes FBI report are missing.)[200]

        "Hold him, Hold him!
        We don't want another Oswald,"

                exclaimed Unruh.[201]

Johnson Took Sirhan's .22 Home

Rafer Johnson took the gun, bringing it home
with him, where he wrote the gun number in his diary.

Around two hours after the shooting, Johnson
brought the revolver to the police,

handing it to Sgt. Michael McCann
                of LAPD-Homicide, in the presence
                of Sgt. R.L. Calkins.

The tape recording of the handover:
McCann: We have an Iver—
Calkins: Iver-Johnson—
McCann: Iver-Johnson Cadet, model 55-A.
Calkins: More of these goddamn guns kill more people—
McCann: Model number 50—number 56-SA. The
serial number is H53725.

(As Lisa Pease points out, "The gun in evidence today
is an Iver-Johnson Cadet, Model 55-SA. Iver-Johnson Model 56-A
(as indicated by Sgt. McCann reading it apparently from the
revolver handed over by Rafer Johnson), however, is a starter gun
that fires blank cartridges.")[202]

Other Victims in the Kitchen Area

Paul Schrade, official with the United Auto Workers union,
                shot in the head;
William Weisel, working for ABC, hit in the abdomen;
Ira Goldstein, reporter for Continental News Service, not serious;
Irwin Stroll, campaign worker, bullet to the leg;
Elizabeth Evans, artist and political activist, superficial wound.

Fred Dutton Removed RFK's Shoes

Dutton, after the speech, had trailed RFK
then heard a "snapping noise, similar to the
                sound of fire-crackers."
He saw RFK on the floor "and he proceeded
        to open his collar and belt,
            removing his cuff links and shoes."[203]

Juan Romero Kneels by Robert Kennedy

Working in the kitchen and pantry
was young Juan Romero,

who wanted to shake Kennedy's hand
(as he had the night he'd delivered
        a cart of food to Kennedy's room)
and pressed through the
                packed pantry.

Romero: "I knew he was about to leave the Embassy Room
and that he would pass through the hallway near the kitchen . . .
I had shaken hands with Senator Kennedy on two previous occasions.

"Is everyone all right?"

"I took a position in the hallway just in front of the opening that leads to the kitchen. There were approximately 15 to 20 people in the hallway. Senator Kennedy came through the door accompanied by approximately five men. He seemed to recognize me. I was smiling and Senator Kennedy was smiling. He held out his hand and I shook it. Senator Kennedy kept walking for approximately one or two steps.

"I continued to observe him and I noticed a man who was to my left and who was smiling and who appeared to be reaching over someone in an effort to shake Senator Kennedy's hand.

"At about the same time I heard gunfire and I noticed that this individual was holding a gun in his hand (which hand not recalled) and that the gun was approximately one yard from Senator Kennedy's head.

"I observed Senator Kennedy placing his hands to his face and he staggered backward a few steps and slumped to the floor.

"I immediately turned my attention completely to Senator Kennedy and I ignored the gunman. I knelt on the floor at Senator Kennedy's left side and I placed my right hand under his head and slightly lifted his head. At this time I felt blood in my right hand.

"I said, 'Come on Mr. Kennedy you can make it.' His lips moved and he seemed to say, 'Is everybody all right.'

"I heard someone say, 'Throw that gum away
Mr. Kennedy,' and I noticed he was chewing gum and I started
to reach for the gum but did not as I did not want to put my fingers
in his mouth. His right eye was wide open
            and his left eye was opening
                and closing."[204]

> By then, Ethel had rushed to the scene
> & then pushed Juan away.
> He asked if he could give Bobby
>   his rosary beads.
>
> "I pressed them into his hand
> but they wouldn't stay . . . so I tried
>   wrapping them around his thumb.
> When they were wheeling him away,

Act of Contrition

I saw the rosary beads
                still hanging off his hand."

Rosary Beads

Daniel Curtain
had worked that day driving voters
                to the polls.

He'd watched RFK's speech,
then followed him
                into the kitchen area.
He told the FBI he was about 15 feet behind Kennedy
just about to go through the swinging doors.

He told the FBI he jumped through the doors
in time to see RFK fall to the floor.

He dashed to RFK's side, telling the FBI
he was among the first, if not the first
                to reach RFK's side.

Curtain "immediately handed Senator Kennedy
a string of rosary beads. Curtain said Kennedy
immediately clutched the beads as Curtain
                placed his lips near Kennedy's ear
                and began an
                        Act of Contrition Prayer."[205]

Dr. Stanley Abo
an LA radiologist
summoned from the
crowd
        found RFK
        holding a cross & beads.

He placed his ear next to the victim's chest.
The breathing was very shallow.
He took his pulse, then stuck a finger
into RFK's head wound "to relieve the" built-up "pressure."

Dr. Stanley Abo feeling the extent of the wound

The wound bled gravely.

"You're doing good," Abo told the Senator.

"The ambulance is on the way."

"O Ethel, Ethel"
    said the man who would have been President,
    softly.[206]

More from Dr. Stanley Abo to the FBI

"When he touched the Senator's face his left eye
opened and he looked at the doctor with a look
that the doctor interpreted as being one of
                    wondering who I was."
The doctor stated that when he saw the Senator's eye
open, and what seemed to him to be a comprehending
look, he spoke to him and told him that Mr. Schrade
appeared to be all right. Dr. Abo stated that
Senator Kennedy appeared to understand this statement
and once again closed his left eye.

"Dr. Abo stated that he explored briefly the wound
in the Senator's head behind his ear and several times
probed the wound slightly in an attempt to prevent
a build up of 'cranial pressure.' He stated that he did
no other active treatment of the Senator but that
during the time he was there, his main goal was to
determine the Senator's state of consciousness,
and to keep other people from attempting to touch the
Senator, or administer any kind of aid to him.

"Dr. Abo further advised that, a very few moments after
he had made this initial brief examination, Senator
Kennedy's wife, Ethel, walked up to him and gave
him a bag of ice which he applied to the Senator's head.
He stated that at this time the Senator
    once again opened his eye and seeing his wife,
    he said 'Oh, Ethel' and reached up slightly
        and grasped her hand and held it."[207]

"Oh, Ethel."

Glancing at His Watch

The writer Pete Hamill, who'd written the letter back in January
   urging RFK to run, looked at his watch:
                                it was 12:15 a.m.

Meanwhile, the video of events in the ballroom
showed that just about 2 and 1/2 minutes after RFK
               left the podium
the ballroom was still packed
when suddenly there were screams, shouts
               & consternation in the audience.

The podium was still overcrowded.
The microphones were still on,
and a minute later a voice is heard:
"What happened, do you know?"
Second voice: "Somebody said he'd been shot."

A few seconds later a young man speaks into the mike:
"Please stay back. Please stay back. . . .
"If there's a doctor, come right here.
From a young man at the other microphone:
"Would a doctor come right here?!"
First microphone: "We need a doctor right here at the microphone,
    immediately!"

Then, a few seconds after that
a man with a Kennedy accent took the mike:
        "Quiet please. Quiet please
        The best thing everybody can do here
        is in an orderly way leave."
        (makes a sweeping gesture with his arm)

        Would you please do that.
        Just in an orderly way clear the room."

        Soon he said "We don't know what's happened
        but all of this noise and confusion
                is not going to help.
        Please clear the room."

Can we in an orderly way
clear the room, please."

"Would you move out quickly."

> "Would you
> please clear
> the room
> in an
> orderly fashion?"

This was followed, a little more than six minutes
after RFK left the stage,
> with "We've got a doctor now.
> Would you please clear the room
> and offer your prayer."

Polka-Dot Races Down the Fire Escape with a Man Wearing a Gold Sweater

Sandra Serrano, RFK campaign worker,
> still was sitting on the fire escape
> below the southwest corner of the Embassy Ballroom

(where RFK was speaking).

She heard what sounded like a car backfiring six times—
then the girl in the polka-dot dress
> and the "Mexican American man" wearing
> a gold sweater "burst out onto the hotel fire escape
> and ran down the stairs, almost stepping on her.

"'We've shot him! We've shot him!' the girl exclaimed.
'We've shot Senator Kennedy!'

After hearing the polka-dot so excited about shooting RFK,
Serrano went back inside and noticed a guard wearing a gray
> uniform "just inside the door, one floor below the pantry."

"'Is it true they shot him?' she asked.
"'Shot who?' asked the guard
"'Senator Kennedy.'

"The guard looked at her like she was crazy, then spotted a glass in her hand. 'I think you've had a little too much to drink, honey.'

"But Serrano couldn't be shaken from what she'd heard. She ran to a public phone booth and dialed her parents in Ohio, collect, long-distance. Crying and near complete hysteria, she launched into a garbled account as a girl she recognized approached the glass.

"'Has Kennedy been shot?' Serrano asked.
Yes, Kennedy had been shot."[208]

(Sandra Serrano, shortly after the woman in the polka-dot dress ran outside, went on live television with NBC reporter Sander Vanocur:

Serrano: "The girl came running down the stairs in the back, came running down the stairs and said, 'We shot him. We shot him.' and I said, 'Who did you shoot?' and she said, 'We shot Senator Kennedy.' . . . She was Caucasian. She had on a white dress with polka dots. She was light-skinned, dark hair. She had on black shoes, and she had a funny nose."[209]

Vincent DiPierro recalled the woman in the polka-dot dress as having a peculiar "pudgy" nose.[210]

A Police Officer Arrives

A block from the Ambassador, LAPD Sergeant Paul Sharaga had stopped to purchase cigarettes.

Getting back into the patrol car, he heard a radio call about a shooting at 3400 Wilshire, which he recognized as the Ambassador.

He sped to the rear of the hotel. In the parking lot he found a couple who very very upset: The woman was in her mid/late 50s, led in the conversation: she said they had been located near the exit stairs,

"We've shot him."

when a young woman and young man ran past "shouting gleefully, "'We shot him! We shot him!'"

The young woman was wearing a polka-dot dress.

"Who did you shoot?"

"Senator Kennedy," replied she in the polka-dot, "We shot him! We killed him!"

The young man and woman, "laughing," then disappeared out of sight in the lot.[211]

Other Witnesses to Polka-Dot Coming Down the Fire Escape

A group of Kennedy supporters, also singers, came to the Ambassador Hotel at 9:30 p.m. (to what the FBI report called "the Grand Ballroom") including Winnie Marshall. There were about 9 singers. "She (Winnie Marshall) stated that they were on the stage most of the evening singing Kennedy songs and generally mixing with the crowd.

"She stated that about 11:50 p.m. or midnight her husband Chris had left the stage and moved to a smaller side room. She stated that while he was going to this other room he passed a fire escape area. She stated that while he was near the fire escape, either he or Gerie McCarthy, who had accompanied him, observed a girl and a young man come down the fire escape shouting, 'They've shot him.' Mrs. Marshall stated that Gerie had told her the girl had worn a polka dot dress and had been saying, 'Kennedy has been shot.'

"Mrs. Marshall stated she did not immediately learn of the shooting until her husband came back to the stage and told her Kennedy had been shot. She advised that the situation was such in the ballroom that it was difficult to hear anything over the noise and that the first official knowledge that anyone there had was when an unknown woman came to the stage and made an announcement that Kennedy was wounded. She stated that immediately after that police came into the Grand Ballroom area and requested that everyone quietly leave the ballroom and they also took all of the balloons away from the crowd.

"Mrs. Marshall stated that about 20 minutes after this happened, Paul went to the Embassy Room which was immediately above the Grand Ballroom. She advised that he later told her about the confusion but that he had not seen anything except one woman who had appeared to be shot."[212]

Footage Showing David Morales Emerging from the Pantry Where RFK Had Been Shot

On page 454 of *Who Killed Bobby?* author Shane O'Sullivan noted that,
"At 12:47, Morales emerged from the pantry
(where RFK had been shot at 12:15)
and walked into the ballroom among a group of police officers.

"At 1:03, 'Morales' is observed comparing notes with someone who looks like a plainclothes detective, though, according to the LAPD, no police were present at the time RFK was shot.

"If Joannides, Campbell and Morales were Bulova executives, they did not act as if they were Bulova executives."

(Recall that Rabern told O'Sullivan he had also observed the man others identified as Campbell in and around the LAPD
"probably half a dozen times,"
as Shane reports in *Who Killed Bobby?* (page 441).

Sirhan Asked Why Why Why?

While Sirhan was being held
George Plimpton asked him why he did it.
No reply.[213]

Jimmy Breslin

Writer Jimmy Breslin
    was on hand in the kitchen.
"Breslin standing very close to Sirhan and
being face-to-face with him, asked him twice
    'Why did you have to do it?'
Sirhan's eyes were rolling
    and he did not answer."[214]

Sirhan Taken Out of the Pantry

Two LAPD patrolmen (Travis White and Arthur Placencia)
arrived at the shooting scene.

Sirhan was pinned to a table.

Another police officer, Randolph Adair, also
had rushed to the scene.

Sirhan, he noticed, "had a blank, glassed-over look on his face
—like he wasn't in complete control of his mind at the time."
(see Dan Moldea book, pages 47–48)

The policemen began to pry Sirhan free from
the grasp of those holding him down.

Jesse Unruh was one of those holding Sirhan
in his grasp, and accompanied the officers
after they handcuffed Sirhan
and brought him down
    through a hostile crowd
        to the squad car.

Unruh jumped into the front seat
while angry citizens pounded on the car;
they switched on the siren
and pulled away
with Officer Placencia reading Sirhan his rights,
Sirhan refusing to give his name.

Who are you? Placencia asked Unruh.
I'm Jesse Unruh.
Who did he shoot? asked the officer.
Bobby Kennedy, replied Unruh.[215]

Jesse Unruh Then

"accompanied the police officers in the car
Sirhan was in to the Rampart Division. He sat in front
with the driver and Sirhan was in the back between
                    two other police officers.

"Around the time they entered the car,
Sirhan mumbled, 'I did it for my country,'
                    according to Mr. Unruh.

"He (Unruh) could not recall at just what point he (Unruh)
asked the question during the ride, but since Sirhn
looked like a Latin-American he asked Sirhan,
                    'Why him? Why him?
                    He was trying to do something.'

"Sirhan muttered, 'It's too late, it's too late.'
He also recalls Sirhan saying,
                    'I can explain, I can explain.'"[216]

Medical Attendants Arrive

Two men in uniforms "like police officers" arrived,
each with a shoulder patch that read "medical attendant"
            to drive Robert Kennedy to the Central Receiving Hospital.

They placed a blanket under him
and began to put him upon a stretcher.

"No, please don't. Don't lift me up," said Robert Kennedy.

The two attendants "heaved" him onto the stretcher
& then "they bumped and banged their way . . . to the elevator."

Pete Hamill looked at his watch again—it was 12:32.
It had taken 17 minutes
            to get Kennedy toward the hospital

He also glanced at the floor.
So much blood where his upper body had lain.
                                    Could he survive?[217]

Dr. Abo Recalls the Ambulance Attendants

            The Doctor told the FBI that approximately
                    15 or 20 minutes
            after he first tended to RFK in the kitchen

            ambulance attendance arrived "and began to
            move him onto the stretcher.
                    He stated that as they did this,
                    the Senator once again opened his left eye
                    and moaned loudly, saying, 'No, no, oh no.'"

            Dr. Abo stated that it was his opinion
            that during the entire time that he was with
            Senator Kennedy, the Senator was conscious
            and at least partly comprehending what was said
            to him and what was happening. He stated that
            the Senator's condition was not what he would describe
            as good but that his condition did not deteriorate
                        during the time
                        that the doctor was with him."[218]

Rosemary Clooney

The great singer Rosemary Clooney,
who had ridden back in the plane with Robert & Ethel
after the final rally in San Diego on Monday,

was in the Ambassador's Embassy Room
when she heard the screams of the shooting
            and sank to her knees.

Last ride

She rushed to the street
clutching her rosary, praying with all her heart
just as RFK was placed
in the ambulance.

Kill Squad Takes Off in Lightless Helicopter from Ambassador Helipad just as Ambulance Bearing RFK Leaves the Hotel?

Mrs. Patricia Stewart, of Maryland, was on hand registered
at the Ambassador Hotel on June 4, 1968.
She is the wife of reporter Richard Stewart.

Her husband was at a television studio in Burbank, California,
the night of the assassination. Patricia Stewart spent the evening
and night in her room at the Ambassador watching the
"campaign activities on television."

"The only thing that she noted which should would consider unusual
was a party in an adjoining room which was very noisy,
and which continued to be so even
after the word of the assassination of Senator Kennedy
was publicized on radio and televsion.

"SHE ALSO FELT THAT IT WAS UNUSUAL WHEN
A HELICOPTER ON THE HELICOPTER PAD AT THE HOTEL
LEFT JUST AFTER THE AMBULANCE LEFT THE HOTEL
WITH, PRESUMABLY, SENATOR KENNEDY, AND THE
HELICOPTER DID NOT PUT ITS LIGHTS ON UNTIL
IT REACHED AN ALTITUDE OVER THE BUILDING."[219]

Good Samaritan Hospital

The emergency doctors at Central Receiving
restored his breathing
then soon transferred him to Good Samaritan Hospital

where the great Senator lingered
in life through the next day
and into the next night.

Too many bullets

Walter Cronkite, Early A.M.

CBS newsman Walter Cronkite
broadcast to the nation
        early in the a.m.

Cronkite read LAPD Police Chief Thomas Reddin's
brief statement
        that the suspect had not yet been identified
        & had not made any statement.

Cronkite then went on to describe the shots fired:
"He apparently fired all of the eight shots
in the magazine of a .22 caliber revolver,
those shots taking effect in Senator Kennedy
and four other persons, as far as we
        have been able to determine,
with some still rather confused reports and
        incomplete identification
        of all the others wounded.

"One witness said that those shots came
so close together that he could scarcely believe
they were fired from one gun. A reporter heard the
shots from an adjoining room, and they sounded
almost as if they came from a machine gun,
        so short was the bursts of fire."[220]

RFK Passes Away

Los Angeles Coroner Thomas Noguchi
prepared a team to perform the autopsy.

"At 6:30 p.m. on Wednesday (June 5)," Noguchi later stated,
"the hospital informed us that the Senator
had a flat electroencephalogram, so we knew
        the end was near."

RFK left life at 1:44 a.m. on Thursday, June 6,
and then at 3 a.m. Noguchi began the autopsy.

For some reason three military pathologists
were flown in from DC to witness it. Why?

The Fatal Bullet Fired from Two or Three Inches Away

One key finding of Noguchi's investigation:
"powder burns around the entry wound indicated that the fatal bullet
was fired at less than one inch from the head and no more than two or
three inches behind the right ear."

> CIA Counterintelligence Chief James Angleton
> & FBI head J. Edgar Hoover
> both kept photographs of RFK's autopsy
> in their private files.[221]

A Goal: Keep the Bullet Count Down

> They needed to keep the bullet count down
> to no more than
> could have been fired by Sirhan Sirhan
> i.e., eight.
>
> So, they had to deprecate, denigrate and erase
> all assertions that there were bullets
>
> found in the center post of the double doors
> leading into the killing zone.

FBI Agent William Bailey on the Bullet Holes in the Center Post

Retired FBI officer William Bailey told Vincent Bugliosi
in 1975 that he "had worked at the RFK crime scene and
definitely saw what appeared to be bullets lodged in the door frame.
At least two holes in the center post, he later said.

Bailey later said, "I looked into these holes. . . . They were
definitely not nail holes. There appeared to be objects inside."[222]

Uecker and the Holes

Karl Uecker returned to the crime scene the morning
of June 5, 1968, and noticed two holes, not seen previously,
in the center post.[223]

Bullets in Sirhan's DeSoto

The police found two spent bullet tips in the glove compartment
with wood frags on them. Melanson wonders if they weren't
the two dug out of the pantry door frame, and placed, as a
deceit, into
the DeSoto.[224]

June 5, Middle of Night

In night's midst
RFK to 9th floor of
　　　Good Samaritan
and operated on
by a team of 3 surgeons.[225]

Morning of June 5

Sirhan's brother Munir
went to work
in downtown Pasadena
　　　at a department store.

He saw a bunch of fellow workers
around a TV.

He learned that RFK was shot,
stopped to gaze
& the image of the yet-unidentified
shooter
　　　came on the screen.

It was his brother.
Munir drove home,

**Kennedy children leaving the Beverly Hills
Hotel the next day**

informed his older brother, Adel,
then he drove Adel to Pasadena police headquarters
arriving around 9:15 a.m.[226]

Adel returned to the house at 696 Howard Street
with a group of police.

By the time they arrived
LA mayor Sam Yorty had already
gone on television to announce the shooter was Sirhan Sirhan
& giving the media his home address.

There were media already outside when Adel Sirhan
and the officers arrived.

They were shown Sirhan Sirhan's bedroom
in the back of the house,

where they found Rosicrucian literature
"as well as many other books on the occult"

and two spiral notebooks
one on a dressing table
       & another on the floor
              by Sirhan's bed

(no mention in official records on what happened
to Sirhan's shortwave radio apparatus).[227]

LAPD Command Post

The RFK investigation
command post
       became the LAPD's Ramparts Station house.[228]

Within a few days, the Los Angeles Police Department
had formed the SUS unit

      or "Special Unit Senator,"
      which handled the investigation of the case.

Dr. Thomas T. Noguchi's Autopsy and the Trouble for Him It Caused

Thomas Noguchi, "Chief Medical Examiner-Coroner" of LA County,
performed an exhaustive autopsy on RFK
>>beginning at 3 a.m. on June 6
>>& lasting for 6 hours

at Good Samaritan Hospital,
>>resulting in a 62-page report

titled "Medicolegal Investigation on the Death of
>>Senator Robert F. Kennedy."[229]

Noguchi later told a magazine:
"Senator [Edward] Kennedy was eager to have the body flown back
to Washington immediately. But I insisted that this
was no time to rush. And he finally agreed."[230]

Noguchi: "The Senator was shot late on a Tuesday night after
delivering a victory speech in the Ambassador Hotel.
Shortly afterward, my duty staff called me at home and
notified me of the sad event. From then on, my office
was in constant contact with the Good Samaritan Hospital,
where the Senator had been taken, and I assembled the team that
I wanted to assist me in the autopsy. At 6:30 p.m. on Wednesday,
the hospital informed us that the Senator had a flat
electroencephalogram, so we knew the end was near. I met
with members of the Kennedy family in the district attorney's office
to work out procedures. Death came at 1:44 a.m. on Thursday
morning, and I went straight to the hospital. At 3 a.m., after the
preliminary x-ray and fluoroscopic examinations were completed,
I started the autopsy."[231]

>>Noguchi: "I was very fond of Kennedy, and when
>>I first saw him on the autopsy table, he
>>looked exactly as he had when I saw him
>>on television. He looked as if he were
>>still alive. I asked my assistants to
>>cover his face."[232]

Six hours of carve—
only RFK's
limbs were
left intact.[233]

The Bullet That Killed Had Been Fired
Three Inches from RFK's Mastoid
(One Inch Behind the Edge of the Ear)

The first question Noguchi asked when he was shown
Kennedy's body was, "Where are the hair shavings?"
The surgeons who had operated on Kennedy had partially
shaved his head, and Noguchi knew, or suspected,
these hair shavings could contain critical evidence.

"I had such admiration for him, such hope that he would
become President, that I did not want to be influenced
by my feelings." Noguchi discovered that one bullet
had passed through Kennedy's right armpit, another—

which he recovered—had lodged in his spinal column,
while a third—the one that killed him—had penetrated
his skull just to the left of his right ear and subsequently
shattered.

A day after he'd done the autopsy, Noguchi was called
by a criminalist at the LAPD who said that soot had been found
in the hair shavings. "I really sat up in my chair when I heard that.

"This was a very important discovery because all the witnesses
had reported that the gunman [Sirhan Sirhan] had been at least
a yard away from Kennedy when he shot him.

"But soot meant that a gun had been discharged from a
much closer range."

To the surprise of his colleagues, Noguchi asked if he could be
provided with seven pigs' ears. Once these had been fetched
from a local butcher, he took them to the Police Academy

Broken Glory

for ballistics tests. The patterns of soot on the pigs' ears suggested that the shot that killed Kennedy had been fired from just three inches away.[234]

"We know that the three gunshot wounds were at close range. I had my staff construct a likeness of Kennedy's head and attach pig ears to this model, which was covered with cloth to absorb gunpowder. We hoped to create identical powder tattooings found at the edge of the right ear by using the suspected weapon and by shooting from various distances into the right mastoid. Moving away by distances of an inch, only when the muzzle was three inches behind the mastoid, around one inch behind the edge of the ear, did I get the exact duplicate of the actual death-shot powder tattoo. We also did infrared photography and X rays of the bits of hair taken from around the wound. This determined the powder spread and confirmed the pig ear test.

"When I testified before the grand jury, the deputy D.A. said, 'You mean three feet?' I said, 'No, three inches.' And he said, 'If you made a mistake, you can still change it.' But I said [laughs], 'I'm not going to change it.'"[235]

Military Personnel on Hand at the Autopsy

"Consultants from the Armed Forces Institute of Pathology:

Pierre A. Finck
Colonel, MC, USA
Chief, Military Environmental Pathology Division and
Chief, Wound Ballistics Division

Charles J. Stahl, III
Commander, MC, USN
Chief, Forensic Pathology Branch and
Assistant Chief, Military Environmental Pathology Division

Kenneth Earl, M.D.
Chief, Neuropathology Branch."[236]

Fatal Shot Just Several Inches away
from Back of Head
—from Noguchi's actual Autopsy Report

A series of firings was then performed using geometry simulatin
that of the fatal gunshot wound to the head, as determined by
previous studies. The post-auricular region was simulated by
the padded muslin described above. The ear was simulated by an
animal ear obtained from an abbatoir and with the hair removed.

With the test weapon at an angle of 15·degrees upward and
30 degrees forward (to correspond with goniometric data) and
at a distance of one inch (2.5 cm) from the edge of the right
"ear," the test pattern is most similar to the powder residue
pattern noted on the Senator's right ear and on hair specimens
studied. Similarity persists, on the 2 inch (5 cm) distance
firing, with respect to the distribution of discrete powder gra

        which makes it impossible for
        Sirhan Sirhan
            to have fired fatally.

Noguchi Testifies at Grand Jury Hearing

At the RFK grand jury on June 7, 1968,
Deputy District Attorney John Miner
asked Coroner Noguchi
   what was "the maximum distance the gun
      could have been from the Senator
      and still have left powder burns?"

Noguchi replied, "Allowing for variation, I don't think it
will be more than two or three inches from
      the edge of the right ear."

Uh oh—the conspirators couldn't allow
      the fatal gunshot to have occurred
      from a gun other than Sirhan's,
       which was nowhere near the back of RFK's head.

Noguchi later revealed
    that before going in to testify before the Grand Jury
    a deputy DA approached him
        to ask him to change the 1–3 inches
        for the fatal shot
           to one to three feet.

Noguchi refused.[237]

(Two months after Noguchi's testimony
"Noguchi's office was publicly accused of 'deficiencies'
that caused murders to go 'undetected' and suicides to
be 'mislabeled.'")[238]

CIA Counterintelligence Chief
Involved in Campaign to Discredit Noguchi?

We have noted that CIA Counterintelligence chief,
the baleful James Angleton,
kept a set of the grim RFK autopsy photos
in his CIA safe, plus also
some files on the RFK hit.

(Maybe Angleton helped set up or coordinated
the campaign to ruin the career of
LA Coroner Thomas Noguchi.)[239]

More on Grand Jury
June 7

"Criminologist (Dwayne) Wolfer testified about the gun . . .
at a grand jury hearing. His expert testimony was that a bullet
removed from the area of Kennedy's sixth
cervical vertebra
and another taken from William Weisel's
abdomen had been fired by the
Iver-Johnson revolver.

"Four of the seven test bullets which Wolfer indicated
were fired from Sirhan's gun and reclaimed were introduced
as Exhibit 5B.

"At Sirhan's trial—months later—Wolfer said that
Sirhan's gun had fired the Kennedy and Weisel evidence
bullets. Three test bullets used for comparison
were introduced as Exhibit 55.

"The envelope holding the bullets was marked with
the gun serial number H18602—not H53725, the number
of Sirhan's gun. The wrong number was not discovered
until nearly two years later.

"Pasadena criminologist William W. Harper, a sometime
critic of Wolfer's work, noted it in November 1970,
while checking physical evidence in the case
at the county clerk's office."[240]

Saying Goodbye in a Cathedral
June 7, 1968

Robert Kennedy was flown to New York City.
His casket was on view in St. Patrick's Cathedral
on 5th Avenue
on June 7.

The public was allowed in around 5:30 a.m.

Hundreds had waited through the night.

By day's end 151,000 had walked
past his casket.

The Funeral and Burial,
Saturday, June 8

The funeral was held at St. Patrick's
and lasted one hour and forty-five minutes.

Ted Kennedy delivered the eulogy, ending:

"My brother need not be idealized or enlarged in death
beyond what he was in life. He should be remembered
simply as a good and decent man
who saw wrong and tried to right it,
saw suffering and tried to heal it,
saw war and tried to stop it.

"Those of us who loved him and who take him
to his rest today pray that what he was to us,
          and what he wished for others,
                    will someday come to pass for all the world.

"As he said many times in many parts of this nation
to those he touched and who sought to touch him:
          'Some men see things as they are and say why.
          I dream things that never were and say why not.'"

Then his mahogany coffin
          traveled by black-draped train to Washington
                    to be buried in Arlington National Cemetery.

Two Sets of Forlorn Eyes at the Funeral

On the sidewalk outside St. Patrick's
Richard Goodwin,
          whom RFK had asked to come to Frankenheimer's
          Malibu house to confer on Victory Day

          & then had helped write his victory statement,

locked eyes
with a very forlorn John Frankenheimer,

          also standing outside the church.

Frankenheimer who had set aside his powerful career
for 102 days straight
          to film and put together television ads & interviews
          with RFK

          & had been waiting outside the hotel with Evans
          to drive Bob and Ethel to the Factory

—locked eyes

Goodwin recalled: "He waved to me. He did not smile,
          nor did I.
          We were not to smile again
                    for a long time."

344

Funeral train

Devastated, drinking in excess, John moved to France
for a while,
>   where he and Evans
>   studied French together

& only after years could he really rebegin his career.[241]

Ceaselessly Working to Limit the Investigation

Both the LAPD's SUS, "Special Unit Senator,"
and to some extent the FBI,
>   worked without cease
>   to limit the investigation.

They had to keep the total number of bullets at 8
& to assert all eight bullets were fired by Sirhan

and that all the wounds in the victims
>   RFK, Paul Schrade, William Weisel,
>   Ira Goldstein, Irwin Stroll, & Elizabeth Evans,

>   had to come from Sirhan's gun

& to pooh pooh the woman in the polka-dot dress
& in general any assertion that Sirhan had not
>   acted alone.

Reputable researchers claim
that as early as Sirhan's trial in '69
the prosecution
>   allowed substitute bullets into evidence
>   instead of the real bullets,
>   & the defense accepted the bullets without analysis
>   which altered history.[242]

Then in 1971 criminologist William Harper
gained access to both
>   the bullet from RFK's neck
>   & the bullet lodged in William Weisel's abdomen
>   (Weisel was several feet behind RFK)

and, utilizing a new instrument called the
      Hycon Balliscan camera,

    he analyzed both bullets,
        including "rifling patterns,"

    and concluded that the bullets
    were fired from two different guns.

    Proving that at least 2 guns were
        fired in the pantry!

It was revealed years later that, unbeknownst to William Harper,
the LAPD had run its own independent analysis
of the two bullets using its own Hycon Balliscan camera.
Criminologist Larry Baggett concluded that:

1. The bullets that hit RFK and William Weisel
    were NOT fired from the same gun.

2. The bullet that entered RFK's neck was not fired
    from Sirhan's revolver.

Then in 1975, after public pressure, seven court-appointed
experts were given the "evidence" bullets to examine—
One of the experts made a listing of the ID markings
contained on the bases of the victim bullets, and it was noted that
the ID markings DIFFERED from the ID engravings
placed on them by the operating surgeons
        in the hospital the night of the shootings.

    Indicating that bullets had been switched.[243]

    —Rose Lynn Mangan
    "The Get Lost Letter," 1-1-16

Imbalance on the Edge

After RFK was murdered,
his closest friends seemed close to insanity;
the grief was like a primitive stack of boulders on the soul.

(The great singer Rosemary Clooney suffered a breakdown
because of the evil.)

The View from Avenue A

Miriam and I watched the returns
      in our apartment on 12th Street & Avenue A
just up the street from the Peace Eye Bookstore.

I was weeping and wondering what to do
on such a violent planet
      and gory nation.

A member of my band, the Fugs, had called RFK
an "amphetamine wolverine" at a concert at the
Fillmore East on Second Avenue,
      the weekend before the primary.

Now I felt devastated
watching the Ambassador on tv,
Up all night, as I pondered changing my life
maybe going to law school
      and devoting myself to a Better World.

Four years later, investigating the Manson
      group's murders,
        I learned some things about the assassination,
which grew, over the decades, into
      this book.

The Feather of Justice

Is there no Justice?
Is there no Ancient Feather of Justice
to judge against
    Evil?

Here's what I believe
occurred by the Ice Machine.

IS THERE NO JUSTICE?
IS THERE NO ANCIENT FEATHER OF JUSTICE?
TO JUDGE AGAINST
              EVIL?

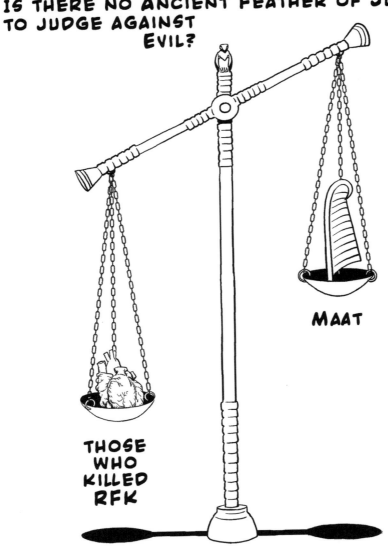

MAAT

THOSE
WHO
KILLED
RFK

I believe that Robert Kennedy
was assassinated
      by one or more US Clandestine Intelligence Agencies,
    probably by the CIA
        or possibly by elements of the Army

& that Sirhan was robo-washed
      by CIA doctors and hypno-warriors
who may have also worked on James Earl Ray
                in LA.

(and here's what I also believe:
The plan
    to kill RFK
by means of a robo-washed killer
patsy
& a close-by hitman
had to have flowed
at least with the knowledge
at the top:

including CIA director Richard Helms.)

Sung

Oh, won't somebody please tell me why
the guns aim so often to the left

    It wounded the nation
    in countless ways,
    wounded her history
    the rest of her days.

    It wounded the future
    Like Lincoln amort
    Or Roosevelt sinking
    and the A-bomb's retort.

    Tell me again why the guns
    always aim to the left?

with gun powder ballots
& voting with knife-heft

never for peace
        always for strife
                empire & war
                        a dollar a life.

Robert Kennedy, he fell down
He fell down by the Ice Machine
By the Ice Machine

With a Rosary in his hand
He lay by the Ice Machine
By the Ice Machine.

Thus history was transgressed
by the snarly men of Fate.
Men of war-mind & racists to boot
like those who killed the Gracchi
of antique Rome.

And so, after JFK, MLK & RFK
the history of the United States
                was irrevocably changed
                      in the direction of violence
                        and transgression.

Notes

1   Douglas, James, *JFK and the Unspeakable: Why He Died and Why It Matters,* Ossining: Orbis Books, 2008. 369–370.
2   Ibid, 380–381.
3   Schlesinger, Arthur M. Jr., *Robert Kennedy and his Times,* New York: Ballantine, 1979. 704–770.
4   Ibid, 710.
5   Heuvel, William Vanden and Milton Gwirtzman, *On His Own: RFK 1964–68,* New York: Doubleday, 1970. 179–180.
6   Schlesinger, *Robert Kennedy,* 718–719.
7   Ibid 728–729.
8   Heuvel and Gwirtzman, *On His Own,* 217.
9   Ibid, 217–218.
10 Ibid, 218.
11 Ibid, 219–220.
12 Ibid, 222–223.
13 Ibid, 225–227.
14 Schlesinger, *Robert Kennedy,* 805.
15 Talbot, David, *Brothers: The Hidden History of the Kennedy Years,* New York: Free Press, 2007. 303–305.
16 Heuvel and Gwirtzman, *On His Own,* 226–227.
17 Kaiser, Robert Blair, *RFK Must Die: A History of the Robert Kennedy Assassination and its Aftermath,* New York: Dutton, 1970. 207–208.
18 Anonymous, Interview by US Federal Bureau of Investigation, Beta RFK/FBI files, 6-8-68. 880–882.
19 Van Antwerp, Edward, Interview by US Federal Bureau of Investigation, #2-2Beta, RFK/FBI files, 6-14-68. 709–710.
20 US Federal Bureau of Investigation, "Sirhan Medical Records," *The Robert F. Kennedy Assassination Archive Collection,* North Dartmouth: University of Massachusetts Dartmouth, 1996. 71.
21 Kaiser, *RFK Must Die,* 207–208.
22 O'Sullivan, Shane, *Who Killed Bobby? The Unsolved Murder of Robert F. Kennedy,* New York: Union Square Press, 2008. 90–91.
23 Skeets, Millard, Interview by US Federal Bureau of Investigation, #3-2 Beta, RFK/FBI files, 10-28-68. 90–91.
24 US Federal Bureau of Investigation, "Sirhan Medical Records," 45.
25 Welch, Terry, Interview by US Federal Bureau of Investigation, #2-2 Beta, RFK/FBI files, 6-11-69. 535–538.

26 *Sirhan Bishara Sirhan v George Galaza, et. al., 2:00-cv-05686-CAS -AJW* (2011) "Exhibit H: Declaration of Dr. Daniel Brown." 20–22.

27 Heuvel and Gwirtzman, *On His Own,* 226–227.

28 Ibid, 227–230.

29 Ibid, 234–237.

30 Schlesinger, *Robert Kennedy,* 827.

31 Cassidy, Bruce and Bill Adler, *RFK: A Special Kind of Man,* Chicago: Playboy Press, 1977. 236–237.

32 Talbot, *Brothers,* 322–323.

33 Heuvel and Gwirtzman, *On His Own,* 240–241.

34 Newfield, Jack, Interview by author, 5-25-76.

35 Talbot, *Brothers,* 314.

36 Heuvel and Gwirtzman, *On His Own,* 277.

37 Ibid, 279.

38 Ibid, 289–290.

39 Ibid, 293.

40 Ibid, 293–294.

41 Sanders, Ed, *America, a History in Verse Vol. 3,* Boston: Black Sparrow Press, 2002. 234.

42 Ibid, 238.

43 Frank, Gerald, *An American Death,* New York: Bantam Books, 1973. 369–371.

44 Fisher, Eddie, *My Life, My Loves,* New York: Harper & Row, 1981. 340.

45 Heuvel and Gwirtzman, *On His Own,* 303.

46 Ibid, 306.

47 Sanders, Ed, *1968: A History in Verse,* 42-43.

48 Ibid, 45-49.

49 Clarke, Thurston, "The Last Good Campaign," *Vanity Fair,* June 2008. 122.

50 Witcover, Jules, *85 Days: The Last Campaign of Robert Kennedy,* New York: G. P. Putnam's Sons, 1969. 113.

51 Ahern, Steven Dale, Interview by US Federal Bureau of Investigation, #4-3 Alpha, RFK/FBI files, 6-6-68. 925–926.

52 Bender, Byron and Neil Swidey, "Robert F. Kennedy Saw Conspiracy in JFK's Assassination," *The Boston Globe,* June 1, 2016. N/p.

53 Just, Ward, *Washington Post,* June 7, 1968.

54 Weidner, John, Interview by US Federal Bureau of Investigation, Gamma, RFK/FBI files, 6-12-68. 210–214.

55 Kaiser, *RFK Must Die,* 216.

56 Heuvel and Gwirtzman, *On His Own,* 258–259.

57 Clarke, "The Last Good Campaign,"114–115.

58 Ibid, 118.

59 Crowe, Walter, Interview by US Federal Bureau of Investigation, RFK/FBI Files, 4-18-69; Peter Noyes, Interview with author, personal communication, 8-8-75.

60 US Federal Bureau of Investigation, Letter from Martin Lee to E. S., "Letters from Marty Lee 1977–1978," RFK/FBI files, 4-24-78. N/p.

61 "Tape #43: Candy Jones," *The Robert F. Kennedy Assassination Archive Collection,* North Dartmouth: University of Massachusetts Dartmouth, 1996. Audiocassette.

62 Ibid.

63 Melanson, Philip, "The Programming of Sirhan Sirhan: Some Additional Data (February 1992)," *The Robert F. Kennedy Assassination Archive Collection,* North Dartmouth: University of Massachusetts Dartmouth, 1996.

64 Turner and Christian, *The Assassination,* 226.

65 Ibid, 228–229.

66 *Sirhan Bishara Sirhan v George Galaza, et. al.,* Exhibit H, 22–23.

67 Ibid, 24.

68 Witcover, *85 Days,* 198.

69 Ibid, 206.

70 Salinger, Pierre, *P.S.: A Memoir,* New York: St. Martin's Press, 1995. 186–188.

71 Schlesinger, *Robert Kennedy,* 968.

72 Stein, Jean and George Plimpton, as cited in: Clarke, Thurston, *The Last Good Campaign: Robert F. Kennedy and 82 Days That Inspired America,* New York: Henry Holt, 2008. 115.

73 O'Sullivan, *Who Killed Bobby?* 162.

74 Noyes, Peter, Interview with author, personal communications, 8-6-75.

75 Article from the *Associated Press,* dated November 23, 1963, as cited in: Noyes, Peter, *Legacy of Doubt.* New York: Pinnacle Books, 1973. 232–233.

76 Witcover, *85 Days,* 221–222.

77 O'Sullivan, *Who Killed Bobby?* 107.

78 Witcover, *85 Days,* 225–226.

79 *Sirhan Bishara Sirhan v George Galaza, et. al.,* Exhibit H, 4–5; see also 22–23.

80 Ibid, 22–23.

81 *Sirhan Bishara Sirhan v George Galaza, et. al.,* 2:00-cv-05686-CAS-AJW (2011), Exhibit I: "Declaration of Dr. Daniel Brown." N/p.

82 Westlake, Dana, Interview by US Federal Bureau of Investigation, #2-1 Kensalt Files, 6-17-68. 3–4.

83 Erhard, George Jr., Interview by US Federal Bureau of Investigation, #2-1 Kensalt Files, 6-7-68. N/p.

84 Ibid.

85 Witcover, *85 Days*, 247.

86 "Tape #43: Candy Jones," *The Robert F. Kennedy Assassination Archive Collection.*

87 Skorcewski, Dawn M., *An Accident of Hope: The Therapy Tapes of Anne Sexton,* Abingdon: Routledge, 2012. Skorczewski notes the following regarding Orne's Viennese accent: "The tapes recorded toward the end of 1963, at which point this book begins, are of a better quality than many of those recorded before that time. Perhaps Orne had purchased new equipment. Sexton's voice sounds stronger, as does Orne's, and both are more audible. Orne's Viennese accent does not seem any weaker over the years, although Sexton's Boston Brahmin tones do seem more modulated. Most of the words on the tapes can be heard perfectly well, complete with Sexton's exclamatory 'Oh, Dr. Orne!' and Orne's protracted 'mmhmmm's.' Some tapes feature the long silences of Sexton's trances, the dissociated states she entered when angry or upset, presumably in an attempt to manage her feelings. We can hear Orne's soothing voice as he attempted to coax her back to consciousness, and the flare of his anger when she refused to do so, even though the appointment had come to an end and another patient was waiting outside."

88 Marks, John, *The Search for the Manchurian Candidate: The CIA and Mind Control,* New York: New York: Dell Publishing, 1988. 172–173, 181.

89 Final report of work carried out under the Office of Naval Research contract NONR-4731(00), June1, 1968–May31, 1971, Martin T. Orne, Institute of the Pennsylvania Hospital, 5-31-71; 86-page report in author's archive.

90 O'Sullivan, *Who Killed Bobby?* 111–112.

91 Kaiser, *RFK Must Die,* 549.

92 Lewis, Roger, Interview by US Federal Bureau of Investigation, #3-1 RFK/FBI Files, 10-11-68. 100.

93 Bruno, Jerry and Jeff Greenfield, *The Advance Man: An Official Offbeat Look at What Really Happens in Political Campaigns,* New York: William Morrow, 1971. 118.

94 Sheridan, Walter, Interview by US Federal Bureau of Investigation, #3-2 Alpha RFK/FBI Files, 10-10-68. 55–56.

95 Scanlon, Joseph, Interview by US Federal Bureau of Investigation, #3-2 Beta RFK/FBI Files, 10-2-68. 264.

96 Los Angeles Police Department, "Addendum for Progress Report of August 2, 1968," *The Robert F. Kennedy Assassination Archive Collection,* North Dartmouth: University of Massachusetts Dartmouth, 1996.

97   Owen, Jerry, Interview by US Federal Bureau of Investigation, Gamma RFK/FBI Files, 7-8-68. 295–301.

98   Witcover, *85 Days*, 247–251.

99   Smith, Peter, Interview by US Federal Bureau of Investigation, #4-1 RFK/FBI Files, 6-18-68. 115.

100 Witcover, *85 Days*, 247–251.

101 Glenn, John, Interview by US Federal Bureau of Investigation, #4-1 RFK/FBI Files, 6-14-68. 94.

102 Kaiser, *RFK Must Die*, 534.

103 O'Sullivan, *Who Killed Bobby?* 214–217.

104 Melanson, Philip, *The Robert F. Kennedy Assassination: New Revelations on the Conspiracy and Cover-Up*, New York: Shapolsky Publishers, 1991. 262–264.

105 Thornburgh, James, Interview by US Federal Bureau of Investigations, #2-1 Alpha RFK/FBI Files, 6-24-68. 40–41.

106 Mangan, Lynn, "Plain Talk 3" www.sirhanresearcher.com, 9-11-2011. http://www.sirhansresearcher.com/plaintalk3.htm.

107 Goodwin, Richard N., *Remembering America: A Voice from the Sixties*, Boston: Little, Brown and Company, 1988. 535–536.

108 Kaiser, Robert, e-mail message to the author, 5-31-2002.

109 Smith, Interview by US Federal Bureau of Investigation, 122.

110 Hacker, Terry, Interview by US Federal Bureau of Investigation, #4-1 RFK/FBI Files, 10-8-68. 177–178.

111 Salinger, *P.S.*, 196.

112 Eppridge, Bill, *A Time It Was: Bobby Kennedy in the Sixties*, New York: Harry N. Abrams, 2008. 9.

113 Thornburgh, Interview by US Federal Bureau of Investigation, 40–41.

114 US Federal Bureau of Investigation, "Chronology of Events in the Life of Sirhan Bishara Sirhan," #3-3II RFK/FBI Files, 12-20-68. 8.

115 Mistri, Gaymoard, Interview by US Federal Bureau of Investigation, Beta RFK/FBI Files, 6-8-68. 869–872.

116 Kranz, Thomas, "Los Angeles County District Attorney's Office Special Counsel Report on the Assassination of Senator Robert F. Kennedy," Los Angeles County Board of Supervisors, March 1977. 12–13.

117 Rabago, Enrique, and Humphrey Cordero, Interview by US Federal Bureau of Investigation, Beta RFK/FBI Files, 6-5-58. 439–442.

118 Cabrillo, Gonzalo, Interview by US Federal Bureau of Investigation, #4-1 RFK/FBI Files, 6-19-68. 31–32.

119 Kranz, "Special Counsel Report," 12–13.

120 *Sirhan Bishara Sirhan v George Galaza, et. al.,* Exhibit H. n/p.

121 Rabern, David, Interview by Shane O'Sullivan. *RFK Must Die!* Soda Productions: United Kingdom, 11-20-2007.

122 Romero, Juan, Interview by US Federal Bureau of Investigation, Kensalt Investigation Files, 6-6-68. 383.

123 Talbot, David, *The Devil's Chessboard: Allen Dulles, The CIA, and the Rise of America's Secret Government,* New York: HarperCollins, 2015. 499–500.

124 Ibid, 501.

125 Ibid, 503.

126 Salinger, Pierre, *P.S.: A Memoir,* 198–199.

127 Manning, David, "Ted Charach's Press Conference: Thane Eugene Cesar's Gun Found," Probe 2:5, 1995. http://www.ctka.net/pr795-2gun.html.

128 O'Sullivan, *Who Killed Bobby?* 329–334.

129 Turner and Christian, *The Assassination,* 193.

130 Melanson, Philip and William Klaber, *Shadow Play: The Murder of Robert F. Kennedy, the Trial of Sirhan Sirhan, and the Failure of Justice,* New York: St. Martin's Press, 1997. 14–15.

131 Justice, John. Interview by US Federal Bureau of Investigation, #4–2 RFK/FBI Files, 6-19-68. 304–305.

132 Akers, Anthony, Interview by US Federal Bureau of Investigation, #3–1 Beta RFK/FBI Files, 11-18-68. 7–9.

133 Fitzgerald, Polly, Interview by US Federal Bureau of Investigation, #3–1 Beta RFK/FBI Files, 11-25-68. 15.

134 Bennett, Ronald T., Interview by US Federal Bureau of Investigation, #2–2 RFK/FBI Files, 6-17-68. 348–352.

135 Bernstein, Fred and Richard Natale, "Director John Frankenheimer's The Manchurian Candidate Plays to a Full House After 26 Years," *People,* 5-16-88. 129.

136 Gardner, William, Interview by US Federal Bureau of Investigation, Beta RFK/FBI Files, 6-8-68. 1058–1060.

137 Timanson, Uno, Interview by US Federal Bureau of Investigation, Gamma RFK/FBI File, 6-12-68. 28–29.

138 Dutton, Fred, Interview by US Federal Bureau of Investigation, #2–3 Alpha RFK/FBI File, 6-26-68. 24–25.

139 Kaiser, *RFK Must Die,* 23–24.

140 O'Sullivan, *Who Killed Bobby?* 169.

141 Marooney, James, Interview by US Federal Bureau of Investigation, #3–2 Alpha RFK/FBI Files, 10-1-68. 45–47.

142 *Sirhan Bishara Sirhan v George Galaza, et. al.,* Exhibit H. 10–11.

143 Smith, Interview by U.S. Federal Bureau of Investigation, 122–123.

144 Kawelec, Stanley, Interview by US Federal Bureau of Investigation, "#56–156 Miscellaneous Documents," Los Angeles Field Office, 6-7-68.

145 Gardner, William, Interview by US Federal Bureau of Investigation, Gamma RFK/FBI Files, 6-12-68. 24.

146 Timanson, US Federal Bureau of Investigation, 28.

147 Unruh, Jesse, Interview by US Federal Bureau of Investigation, #4-1 RFK/FBI Files, 6-14-68. 129.

148 Grier, Roosevelt, Interview by US Federal Bureau of Investigation, Gamma RFK/FBI Files, 6-12-68. 58–63.

149 Rhodes, Nina, Interview by US Federal Bureau of Investigation, #4-2 RFK/FBI Files, 7-15-68. 365–367.

150 Anonymous, Interview by US Federal Bureau of Investigation, #4-1 RFK/FBI Files, 6-14-68. 82–83. Note: Interviewee name withheld by FBI.

151 Kadar, Gabor, Interview by US Federal Bureau of Investigation, #4-2 RFK/ FBI Files, 7-10-68. 308–309.

152 Barry, William, Interview by US Federal Bureau of Investigation, #4-1 RFK/FBI File, 6-14-68. 75–76.

153 Eppridge, William, Interview by US Federal Bureau of Investigation, #4-2 RFK/ FBI Files, 6-19-68. 242.

154 Kearns, Jane, Interview by US Federal Bureau of Investigation, #3-2 Alpha RFK/FBI Files, 10-7-68. 67.

155 Plimpton, George, Interview by US Federal Bureau of Investigation, #4-1 RFK/FBI Files, 6-1-68. 111

156 Wilson, Susie, *Still Running: A Memoir,* Self-Published, 2014. 204.

157 Eppridge, Interview by US Federal Bureau of Investigation, 6-19-68. 241–244.

158 Ibid.

159 Wilson, Jim, Interview by US Federal Bureau of Investigation, #4-2 RFK/FBI File, 6-20-68. 419–420.

160 Melanson, *The Robert F. Kennedy Assassination,* 65.

161 Ibid, 71.

162 *Sirhan Bishara Sirhan v George Galaza, et. al.,* Exhibit I, 8.

163 Ibid, 11–12.

164 *Sirhan Bishara Sirhan v George Galaza, et. al.,* Exhibit H, 14–15.

165 Di Pierro, Vincent, Interview by US Federal Bureau of Investigation, #4-1 RFK/FBI Files, 6-18-68. 39.

166 Johnson, Rafer, Interview by US Federal Bureau of Investigation, #2-2 RFK/FBI Files, 6-13-68. 375–382.

167 Perez, Jesus, Interview by US Federal Bureau of Investigation, #2-1 Beta RFK/FBI Files, 6-14-68. 241–243.

168 Melanson, *The Robert F. Kennedy Assassination,* 228.

169 Freed, Evan, Interview by US Federal Bureau of Investigation, Gamma RFK/FBI Files, 6-7-68, as cited in a signed affidavit by Frank Burns, Jr, 1994. 70–74.

170 Melanson and Klaber, *Shadow Play,* 128–130.
171 Ibid, 130–132.
172 Green, George, Interview by US Federal Bureau of Investigation, Beta RFK/FBI Files, 6-7-68. 403.
173 Green, George, Interview by US Federal Bureau of Investigation, #4–2 RFK/FBI Files, 7-16-68. 259–260.
174 Johnson, Darnell, Interview by US Federal Bureau of Investigation, Beta RFK/FBI Files, 6-7-68. 407–409.
175 McBroom, Marcus, Interview by US Federal Bureau of Investigation, Private Collection, 7-11-68. 1–4.
176 McBroom, Marcus, as cited in: Melanson, Philip and William Klaber, *Shadow Play: The Murder of Robert F. Kennedy, the Trial of Sirhan Sirhan, and the Failure of Justice,* op. cit.
177 Melanson, *The Robert F. Kennedy Assassination,* 124.
178 Ibid, 65.
179 Ibid, 71.
180 Melanson and Klaber, *Shadow Play,* 128–130.
181 Ryan, Denise, "D.C.-based actress Nina Rhodes speaks of Robert F. Kennedy's assassination," *Vancouver Sun* May 7, 2012. N/p.
182 US Federal Bureau of Investigation, "Martin Lee," RFK/FBI Files. N/p.
183 Sprague, Richard, "The Conspiracy to Assassinate Senator Robert F. Kennedy and the Second Conspiracy to Cover it Up." *Computers and Automation,* October 1970. N/p.
184 *Sirhan Bishara Sirhan v George Galaza, et. al.,* Exhibit H, 15.
185 Witcover, *85 Days,* 266.
186 Melanson and Klaber, *Shadow Play,* 7.
187 Kaiser, *RFK Must Die,* 26.
188 Melanson, *The Robert F. Kennedy Assassination,* 65–66.
189 Cesar, Thane Eugene, Interview by US Federal Bureau of Investigation, Gamma RFK/ FBI Files. 75–77.
190 Hamill, Pete, Interview by US Federal Bureau of Investigation, #2–3 Alpha RFK/FBI Files, 8-6-68. 54–56.
191 DiEugenio, James and Lisa Pease, ed., *The Assassinations: Probe Magazine on JFK, MLK, RFK and Malcolm X,* Port Townsend: Feral House, 2003. 602–603.
192 Melanson and Klaber, *Shadow Play,* 8.
193 See Robert Joling and Philip Van Praag's *An Open and Shut Case: How a "Rush to Judgment" Led to Failed Justice in the Robert F. Kennedy Assassination,* JV & Co., LLC, 2008.
194 DiEugenio and Pease, *The Assassinations,* 568.
195 Schlei, Norbert, Interview on KTLA Radio, 6-5-68.

196 Johnson, Rafer, Interview by Los Angeles Police Department, 6-5-68.

197 Mangan, Lynn, "Plain Talk 3."

198 Reguly, John. Interview by US Federal Bureau of Investigation, #3-2 Alpha RFK/FBI Files, 10-14-68. 54.

199 Harwood, Richard, Interview by US Federal Bureau of Investigation, #4-2 RFK/FBI Files, 6-17-68. 274-275.

200 Hughes, Harold, Interview by the US Federal Bureau of Investigation, #4-2 RFK/FBI Files, 6-10-68. 297.

201 Jesse Unruh exclaiming in footage filmed at time of shooting, as seen on "California Primary Special Broadcast" CBS News, 6-5-68. 52:39.

202 DiEugenio and Pease, The Assassinations, 566-568.

203 Dutton, 24-25.

204 Romero, N/p.

205 Curtain, Daniel, Interview by US Federal Bureau of Investigation, #2-3 Alpha RFK/FBI Files, 9-3-68. 70-72.

206 Melanson and Klaber, Shadow Play, 9-10.

207 Abo, Stanley, Interview by US Federal Bureau of Investigation, #4-1 RFK/FBI Files, 7-11-68. 5; Judith Abo, Interview by US Federal Bureau of Investigation, #4-1 RFK/FBI Files, 7-11-68. 10.

208 O'Sullivan, Who Killed Bobby? 21.

209 Melanson and Klaber, Shadow Play, 14-15.

210 Ibid, 14.

211 Ibid, 10.

212 Marshall, Winnie, Interview by US Federal Bureau of Investigation, #4-2 RFK/FBI Files, 6-27-68. 329-331.

213 Plimpton, 112-113.

214 Breslin, Jimmie, Interview by US Federal Bureau of Investigation, #4-1 RFK/FBI Files, 6-20-68. 188.

215 Melanson and Klaber, Shadow Play, 10-11.

216 Unruh, 130-131.

217 Kaiser, RFK Must Die, 34-35.

218 Abo, Stanley, 5; Abo, Judith, 10.

219 Stewart, Patricia, Interview by US Federal Bureau of Investigation, #3-2 Beta RFK/FBI Files, 10-29-68. 206.

220 Cronkite, Walter, "California Primary Special Broadcast" CBS News, 6-5-68. 1:10-29-1:11:04.

221 O'Sullivan, Who Killed Bobby? 424.

222 Melanson, The Robert F. Kennedy Assassination, 50-51.

223 Ibid, 53-54.

224 Ibid, 58.

225 Melanson and Klaber, Shadow Play, 16.

226 Ibid.

227 Ibid, 17.

228 Ibid, 19.

229 *Sirhan Bishara Sirhan v George Galaza et al., 2:00 cv-05686, CAS-AJW* (2011), Exhibit D: "Medicological Investigation on the Death of Senator Robert F. Kennedy." N/p.

230 Noguchi, Thomas, Interview by Donald Carroll, *Qui Magazine* February 1976.

231 Ibid.

232 Ibid.

233 Blumenfeld, Ralph, *New York Post*, 5-20-75. N/p.

234 Preston, John, "Dr Thomas Noguchi: LA Coroner Confidential," *Telegraph UK*, 9-10-2009. N/p.

235 Noguchi, Thomas, Interview by *Astralgia*, www.astralgia.com. Note: Online article has since been taken down.

236 Noguchi, Thomas, "Autopsy Report #68-5731: Senator Robert F. Kennedy," Los Angeles County Department of Medical Examiner-Coroner, 1968. Note: Turner and Christian do not supply article title or author in their book.

237 Article from the *LA Herald-Examiner*, 5-13-74 as cited in: Turner and Christian, *The Assassination of Robert F. Kennedy*, op. cit. 162.

238 Blumenfeld, *New York Post*.

239 Talbot, *The Devil's Chessboard*, 618.

240 Farr, William and John Kendall, "RFK Shooting Questions Persist," *Los Angeles Times*, 7-20-75. N/p.

241 Goodwin, Richard, "Frankenheimer Memorial Tribute," *Director's Guild of America*, 4-30-08. N/p.

242 Mangan, Lynn, "The Get Lost Letter," sirhansresearcher.com, 1-1-16.

243 Ibid.